The Way to Write Poetry

Books by Michael Baldwin:

Poetry:
Voyage from Spring
Death on a Live Wire
How Chas Eggett lost His Way in a
    Creation Myth
Hob
Buried God
Snook

Pedagogic:
Poetry without Tears
Billy the Kid (ed)
Poems by Children (ed)

Stories:
Sebastian and Other Voices
Underneath and Other Situations

Autobiography:
Grandad with Snails
In Step with a Goat

Novels:
A World of Men
A Mouthful of Gold
Miraclejack
The Great Cham
There's a War on
The Cellar
The Gamecock

SERIES EDITOR JOHN FAIRFAX

The Way to Write Poetry

MICHAEL BALDWIN

Elm Tree Books . London

First published in Great Britain 1982
by Elm Tree Books/Hamish Hamilton Ltd
Garden House 57–59 Long Acre London WC2E 9JZ

Reprinted November 1984

Copyright © 1982 by Michael Baldwin

British Library Cataloguing in Publication Data

Baldwin, Michael
   The way to write poetry.
   1. Poetry — Authorship
   I. Title
   808.3   PN1059.A9

   ISBN 0–241–10748–2
   ISBN 0–241–10749–0 Pbk

Printed in Great Britain by
Redwood Burn Limited, Trowbridge, Wiltshire

Contents

But of all the Bugbears . . . none has been more mischievously efficacious than an Opinion that every Kind of Knowledge requires a peculiar Genius, or mental Constitution, framed for the Reception of some Ideas, and the Exclusion of others; and that to him whose Genius is not adapted to the Study which he attempts, all Labour shall be vain and fruitless, vain as an Endeavour to mingle Oil and Water

Samuel Johnson *The Rambler* Number 25

for
Elizabeth Amy Baldwin
in memory

Acknowledgments

The author and publishers would like to thank the following for permission to quote copyright material:

George Allen & Unwin Ltd for *Selected Poetry and Prose* by Alun Lewis;

Carcanet Press for *Apocrypha* from *Selected poems* by Janos Pilinszky, translated by Ted Hughes and Janos Csokits;

Professor Ed Dorn for *Gunslinger;*

Edinburgh University Press for *The Computer's First Christmas Card* from *The Second Life* by Edwin Morgan;

Faber & Faber Ltd for *On This Island* and other short extracts from *The Collected Poems of W.H.Auden; An Eclogue for Christmas* from *The Collected Poems of Louis MacNeice;* and *ABC of Reading* by Ezra Pound;

Faber & Faber Ltd and Farrar, Strauss & Giroux Inc. for *Sigh as it ends . . . . I keep an eye on your* from *Berryman's Sonnets* © 1952, 1967 by John Berryman; *The Ball Poem* from *Homage to Mistress Bradstreet* (published in the USA and Canada in *Short Poems* © 1948 by John Berryman, © renewed 1976 by Kate Berryman); and *Dream Song no. 322* from *His Toy His Dream His Rest* (published in the USA and Canada in *The Dream Songs* © 1965, 1966, 1967, 1968, 1969 by John Berryman);

Faber & Faber Ltd and Harper & Row Inc. for *Wind* from *The Hawk in the Rain* by Ted Hughes;

Robert Graves & A.P.Watt Ltd for *The White Goddess;*

Mel Hardiment for *Land of the Flying Steamrollers;*

David Higham Associates Ltd for *Do not go gentle into that good night* from *The Poems of Dylan Thomas* published by J.M.Dent & Sons;

The Hogarth Press Ltd for Rilke's *Sonnets to Orpheus,* translated by J.B.Leishman;

John Moat for *A Standard of Verse;*

Routledge & Kegan Paul Ltd for *The Poet Speaks* by P. Orr and *The World Still Needs* from *Winter Sun* by Margaret Avison;

The Scottish Academic Press for *Thirty Bob A Week* from *The Poems of John Davidson;*

Martin Secker & Warburg Ltd for *Amends* from *Noth* by Daniel Huws;

Linda Thompson for *Now The Birds Have Gone*

Every effort has been made to trace the copyright holders of extracts quoted in this book. Should any omission have been made, we apologise and will be pleased to make the appropriate acknowledgment in future editions.

Chapter One

But though your talent cannot be denied,
Some may think you would be better occupied
Sitting in the kitchen doing your philately,
Or in the WC, re-writing Lady Chatterley.

Myra Buttle The Sweeniad

1.

I shall need several tongues.

This book is for poets, would-be poets, teachers of creative writing, teachers in general, and — I hope — that small but increasing body of academics — few in England, more numerous in the United States — who are student philosophers of the creative process.

Then there is the general reader. The book that neglects him is likely to decline into a manual or tract. If from time to time I sag towards manifesto — the word is soggy with politics — my excuse is that poetry is my profession and that now, in however fractured a fashion, I must profess it. So you must expect several tongues, moods and voices; but not, I hope, two faces.

The subject of course is a delicate one. Unfortunately there is little enough space in which to be tentative and none in which to be provisional. We must look at the poet's preparation and study, his necessary knowledge and skills, his props and aids, and some of the useful exercises by which he may seek to become their master. We must consider how to capture and nurture the individual poem, and how to gain a continuing insight from the single fact of its making. Then there is the poet's audience, including presses, writing circles and little magazines.

I shall draw on my own practice, as far as I can be rational about it, other poets' practices so far as I can discover them. Then there will be a summary (often with a caveat, sometimes without an imprimatur) of the various stratagems whereby we place ourselves in the way of writing.

> What do you know
> of Love?
> Know? *Nada.* If
> I knew it couldn't be
> Love.
> Even a mortal knows that.
>
> Ed Dorn *Gunslinger*

There are a million ways to write poetry. Let us get that said at the start. But at the centre of all those ways there must be a functioning intelligence. If we do not accept that we may as well not begin. Poetry is not a Holy Place where we leave our intellects tucked into our boots, outside on the pavement. Our daily task may be the dictating of directives, the combing or laundering of tax returns, the collating of display data and print-outs. We dare not suppose that our poems will require less attention from our common sense. They will need much more beside. Poetry is not a dewy activity.

> And will not the words and character of the style depend on the temper of the soul?
>
> Plato *The Republic*

To be a poet implies a change of consciousness. It involves, if you like, the constant practice of a spiritual exercise. It offers, in short, an impenetrable mask for the freak and the fake who overlook — and bid their disciples overlook — the fact that a poet must also write poems.

> He's the most consummate master of vowels and consonants.
>
> T. E. Lawrence on Shakespeare,
> from a letter to Edward Garnett

This book is about writing poems. Yet it cannot ignore the psychological dimension. Everybody can write a poem, at least one, of substance and worth. To achieve this is our least aim. The problem is how to stay the course. It is there for the professional as much as for the tyro. The poet is someone whose life has been sufficiently focused to allow him to realise a coherent body of such poems. Even a child can uncover miraculous fragments; the search is for the entire mosaic.

> Having begun we must go forward to the rough places of the law.
>
> Plato *The Republic*

We are talking about something that goes beyond and is separate from the poet's philosophy. Every writer, every human being, has his philosophy; and, in the case of many a poet we would not be without, the philosophy is pretty small beer. Eliot has reminded us very pithily that we mean something quite different when we speak of the philosophy of a poet than we do when we speak of the philosophy of a philosopher.

What we are discussing is the poet's relationship with what he fancies to be the sources of his achievement. These may lie in his environment, his reading, his craft or his religion. He may feel them to be part of the chemistry of his own head. Wherever he seeks to locate them, the Romantic and post-Romantic poet always treats them with respect, at the very least because, like Dylan Thomas' shepherd who made ritual observances to the moon, he'd be a damned fool if he didn't.

Some poets, perhaps most of the Romantics (it is hardly a well-charted area) go further than the shepherd and seek out, even supplicate, their inspiration. There was Wordsworth composing while walking, Shelley deliberately dizzying himself with noon light in his sun dome, Keats searching for poetry the feminine presence within the word cages of the printed book. Goethe and Yeats (and how many more?) looked for their power in occult practices; Rossetti, Swinburne and Baudelaire in the merely arcane; and numerous others in the use and abuse of drugs and the bottle.

3

It is tempting to regard this as a comparatively modern pheno-
menon, an early onset of decadence. Certainly we do not readily
associate the Augustans or the poets from the Age of Reason with
this quasi-religious behaviour. They sharpened their brains when
they cut their quills (a fine, though imposed ritual) and there was
an end to it.

I wonder. Can we confidently assert that their invocations of the
Muse, whichever one she was, were merely conventional? If so
they practised an empty artifice that contradicted the very Reason
they professed to uphold. At the very least, there must have been a
kinship with the old shepherd, a feeling that a good prayer said
without belief signified as much as belief without prayer.

I remind myself of Pope's peevish months spent scribbling by
mistlight and candlelight at Stanton Harcourt *in a tower,* and fancy
that Reason must have smelled rather different to a sick man in the
early eighteenth century, not quite as dry, especially when the
owls hooted, the geese honked and the swans clicked and flapped.

I am everywhere,
I suffer and move, my mind and heart move
With all that move me, under the water
Or whistling.
                    John Berryman *The Ball Poem*

Whether it is drawn from Reason or some occult dynamo (if
Reason is not an occult dynamo) a poem must be the product of
the whole self — not quite the same, fortunately, as a whole self.
You don't have to have a poet's self to write a poem, any more
than you need to be an athlete to make a prodigious leap out of
danger. But, as the Duke of Wellington said of his firm seat on a
charger, 'By George, sir, it helps.'

So implicit in our talk of cultivating the poem will be the far
more challenging task of bringing on the poet.

Enough of all this psychic buzz. What about technique?

> I like not these spiritual bugs who strive so hard to stink of Eternity that in the end Eternity stinks of them.
> Nietzsche *Also Sprach Zarathustra*

I am a devotee of technique. It is half of any poet's religion, so the second part of this book deals with it in what might be called summarised detail, bearing in mind that it is a subject which deserves its own bible. I shall talk technique with more tongues than any, because technique means different things to different people.

Midway between technique and philosophy there is method. For many it is no more than the intangible fulcrum, the invisible line that draws itself through the point of balance of a very long plank. For myself, and I believe for most artists, method is everything. The plank must balance along its length. Something, immeasurable though it may be to formal scrutiny, must intervene between the conception and the product. It is the conception which interests the philosopher and the psychologist, and the product which occupies the critic. Artists — and the poet is the supreme artist — grapple endlessly with method. If you do not want me to talk about it, then clearly you have no interest in writing poetry, however much you may think you know about reading it. Lest there be any doubt about it, let me say that method, for the poet, is the way into poetry. The analogy will be crude because it is geometric, and may falsify what I feel about technique; but if we can content ourselves by seeing technique as that which has given shape to the poem, both its form and its detail, as a miraculous vessel, a kind of amphora or Keatsian urn that moves in time; and if we can see our inspiration as the tun of wine, then method is the spike and the hammer that lets in the spigot, and the will to wrench the tap and the force to hold it open until enough has flowed. Method is all of this and more. Method is everything. You must expect to read much of method if you read this book, but you will need to do much more than read if you are to acquire any tools, and much more again if you are to discover the will and the force to use them.

4.

You will have to practise, to regard these words as the syllabus of an apprenticeship. An apprenticeship involves a leisurely absorption of a mystery, and consists, all too often, of following around and sweeping floors. When I walk in circles, and where the dust is thickest, there in all likelihood I shall be talking method, however arcane and haphazard the mumble. So be on your toes for method. I am not going to keep on shouting about it. There are no signposts in a workshop. If you find all of this big-headed, then we have reached a modest area of agreement. It is big-headed, it is most humblingly presumptuous of me; but I know of no other way to do it, because I know of no other person who has been foolish enough to speak of such matters at all.

5.

At the very end of this section, I shall give you a small magic test in method to see if your spirit is tacky enough for any mystery or mastery to stick to it. I shall be testing the pair of us all the time. There will be no question numbers and no answers at the back.

Just this once there will be a clue, though. You are going to enhance your sense of yourself, and the key is in memory, always in memory.

First, something practical. Buy a notebook. Keep it with you all the time. Always be prepared to be a poet, have 'parchment and quill about you more urgent than crust or crumb'. Fill it with what you like, but principally the world, your world, reading, thoughts, gossip, a mirror of your today, a summary of your yesterdays. If you have no yesterdays take a walk until you are marooned inside tomorrow, then use your little book like a liferaft. If you drown serve you right. You deserve to drown if you lack yesterdays.

Chapter Two

My manuscript won't go
in my huge Spanish briefcase . . .
I wonder everytime how I manage it
                    John Berryman *The Dream Songs,* Number 332

1.

The first thing is to fill up that notebook with the raw stuff of poems. What sort of stuff it is, and where we prospect for it, depends on who we are and what sort of poet we want to be.

Who we are may become clearer to us as we keep our notebook. Certainly, the more freshly, spontaneously and fully we keep it the more easily will we assemble ourselves. It is, of course, private, quite as secret as the one Jung concealed on an attic beam for fifty years.

All that is important for the moment is that we form and strengthen the habit of storing our ideas in *written* words. A corollary to this is that for just a few minutes a day we grow used to holding our tongues, even if we are doing no more than making notes of those things that were best in our speech. Our speech, our friends' speech, even our interior dialogue and monologue, is full of gold. We must give ourselves the time to dam and sift, not let it all run down the stream.

What sort of poet do we want to be? That surely is more immediate and objective.

It is, but our ideas on the matter are likely to change when we have written our first poem, and to go on changing (as distinct from developing) unless we take the trouble to understand what that poem is.

. . . for our principle is that rhythm and harmony are regulated by words, and not the words by them . . .
                                        Plato *The Republic*

2.

There are two valid descriptions of the poet. In some cultures and
at some points of time he is held to be a master craftsman.
Elsewhere and otherwise he is considered a seer, a lesser (or
greater) luminary from the hierarchy of saints, prophets,
bonshommes or Men of Knowledge and Power. The second
category has already become a list, but that is in the nature of the
category. The first is crisp and brief because it is a denial of what is

supposed to be the gush of the second. But in the end there are only those two descriptions: a poet is either a maker — a *makyr* as Dumbar called him in his famous lament — who carpenters poems like so many musical chairs — or he is one of the elect who finds the Muse (or God) at his ear.

Those who insist on a third category a little lower than picaresque saint, a little higher than drunken bum, (a sort of mossback jongleur or Divine Idiot), are allowing their eye to be diverted by the social gloss. And society in general glosses indiscriminately; a poet can be itinerant and drunken whether *vates* or *makere.*

No, there are only these two approaches to the mystery, however they may vary in text books: the one professes a discipline of the intellect, the other a discipline of the soul. They are not mutually exclusive. Intelligence is a harmonising word. To discipline the intelligence is one way to gladden the soul, and a man who works hard at his craft may still find the Muse at his ear.

The most useful unifying definition, though, is to say that a poet is a person who writes poetry. Let us for the minute, and the day, and the year, concentrate on that.

> Poet is a posthumous title.
>
> Thomas Blackburn

3.

In a moment we are going to open our notebook and find what brims there. Before that, and afterwards, we are going to divert a little money from our bellies and our follies and spend it on our brains. We are going to buy poetry. It is far too precious to lend or to borrow, too precious and too personal. Only a fool or very close friend tells what he is reading. So let us invite the poets in — they don't cost much; invite them in and let them share our table.

While we are about this gentle buying in, let us also find our 'table'. A writer needs his place, his desk, his room, his shed, his sense of somewhere quiet in a corner of the local library, even like Swinburne his dawn bench in the park.

He also needs to be alone. Loneliness is a gift. To be able to use it properly is a major talent.

Wordsworth was often alone, in the true as distinct from the social sense. In the few words quoted above, he challenges us to an entire strategy of self-improvement.

4.

For the moment, the tactic of the notebook. Let me open mine on a few dead echoes, since you promised your own notes the power of privacy.

Since writing 'privacy' I have leafed through three battered volumes of scruff to find a sequence of forgotten scribbles headed *St Michel, Raissac*. I went to the little medieval chapel there to listen to a friend's choir sing a dead composer's carol written in Oc, the language of Southern France and the tongue of the troubadours. The notes call back a few minutes waiting, but 'little remains in my mind' and less on the page.

The first entry reads:

> The faith is . . ., only by paint light,
> Only by candle
>
> God is inside
> (has no cubic capacity)
> needs no fire
> in the slabs' darkness,
>
> Lives in the paint light,
> Licks at the candles,
> Liking the love-light.

My first instinct is to retch at what I have written, the next to expunge it; but I believe in not throwing words away, and even though I ask 'what roots grow out of this stony rubbish,' I know that there must be some root. For a start these words form part, the discardable part, of my verbal snapshot of S. Michel, Raissac.

10

(You see, I write it correctly for you now I am not transposing; and I owe my craft this, at least.) Something more may come from Raissac, and I may need these pointers.

Next, my knowledge of where my work is going and what it comes from, needs some attention from me. In fact, it needs my total attention, all the time. So by the first two lines I can note that I wrote this same idea, and better, twenty years ago. The second 'verse' represents something, not easily discernible in this version, that I have been wrestling with for half my life. I am sure that I have come closer to throwing it in other notebooks and must seek them out. By the last three lines I can place my private black mark. They are derivative and bad.

Overpage I read:

> Church cool like an old bone,
> Like an old sheep's bone
> in the snow's pasture

I don't mind this. It sounds a bit like me. It sounds a bit like the bit of me that sounds like Ted Hughes, so I promise to avoid it on the very good grounds that no girl goes to the party dressed like her friend.

Overpage again (I am a necessary spendthrift with paper, in case anything should turn into a poem) I find:

> The cripple with her bundle of candles
> Sets my brain on fire

and indulge in a little creative action. I cross out 'bundle of', because although true to memory the extra syllables send the line sprawling, and anyway 'cripple' chimes well enough with 'candle' without the let of 'bundle'. Beside the second line I put a question mark. Is the line strong or merely brash? I shall need to suck it many times before I can be certain either way. It is a poor poem that cannot risk a little vulgarity, but I have not got a poem yet, and my notebooks demand that I should pay myself some disciplined attention.

Overpage again I discover what may well be more of the poem, if poem there be:

> Medieval words in the
> Old God Latin
> Catch coming through
> voices out of Oc
> Out of oc oc oc
> which is man's voice crying
> for the pebbles on the moon . . .

Clearly it is time for me to do some real work. So I copy this page and the last page — all nine lines — on to a clean piece of typing paper. This I shall not fold away or forget. The notebook must be treated as a store-house, an intensifier even; but we must not let it become a prison. If we try to keep finished work in a notebook, we become tyrannised by notebook lengths and sizes. Worse, we may try to keep a neat notebook and grow dazzled by the unalterable virginity of the first wild word.

5.

Unless we can remember with the twenty-eight-year-old Wordsworth that poetry is 'an acquired talent, which can only be produced by severe thought' we are always in danger of being dazzled. At least, I am. You see, I believe that the novelist and the poet tend to view words in a different light. I say 'tend to' because clearly the difference in viewpoint and usage is not absolute, and as a novelist and a poet I find myself on difficult ground; but the poet, whether he constructs or invokes, is generally after his own version of glitter, 'the light that never was'; and we have to remind ourselves whenever the eyebeam truckles that all that glisters is not gold. We want our words to sing, and when they do sing we find it easy to overlook that they sing an old or cheap song.

Nor is it a matter of taste, merely, but philosophy and habit. Like most poets I think in words, not ideas (this is a crude way of putting it, but it is a broadly followable proposition). The problem of translating ideas — the abstract, or even mathematical thump of perception — into words is an agonising, impossible process. So without attempting to elevate the glittering phrase above the succinct, I seek to woo those concepts that will come readily expressed. I woo not words, not ideas, but ideas in words, ideas as words.

I have taught myself, if you like, to *listen* to the experience. If I cannot hear it, I don't write it. Or I don't write it as a poem. When I began to write I spent years in pursuit of the image. My poems swallowed metaphors till they were doubled up in costive folds, like pythons gorged on pigs. Then I realised that rhythm was the thing, not necessarily and primarily metre, but the overall pulse in the imagination no less than the syllable that gives shape to an utterance because there is an insistence at its beginning that presages its end. The snake must ripple and move. Today my problem is syntax, the simple grammar of meaning.

I think that is as it should be. Only a very great poet, Milton perhaps, can begin as a poet of ideas. It is possible to have ideas, political, moral, aesthetic — but not initially as a poet. The magic has to be found first. And yet we owe it to such art as we acquire to make it serve ideas, so that ideas may serve it. So I trust that if I hammer away at an idea then I shall be granted a lyric as an occasional reward.

That is the brief history of my method. For the moment, let me repeat: do not write your poem till you start to hear it. If you remember that small piece of advice you will save yourself time, about fourteen years if my own experience is anything to go by. You may find the sound ready-made in your head. You may discover it by listening to the words in your notebook. First read them at speed: is there already a poem wild and running there? Then read them phrase by phrase. A single cluster of syllables may hum in the mind, and provide you with the necessary spoor. To track them to the end you may need to turn quickly to the second half of this book. *If* your few words point you towards a free metre, then I must say at once that the trail needs experience. As a beginning, cling to the idea of the primitive chant, or the psalms, say, and the sonorities of the Old Prayer Book.

One thing will be clear to you. You are not alone in your perplexity. Those two fragments I have just copied from my own notebook do not chime well together. Yet the phrases are much too set to be conveniently diverted into a regular metre. I must work and so must you.

> Culture is, or ought to be, the study and pursuit of perfection.
>
> Matthew Arnold *Culture and Anarchy*

6.

What can I put in my notebook? What can I work on?

Yourself is too glib an answer. Yourself is what you will discover there, not what you will set down.

Try this as an exercise. Think of something or someone that interests you intensely. Now do some research *among written material* about the object of your interest. Literature is a written art, and books are magic artefacts, so it is worth a poet's while to rub his brain in them. If, for example, you are going to write about a particular wall, trace it in the local archives, study its emergence and any changes in its direction in old ordnance maps, the geological and quarry history of its stone, the kiln history of its brick. What is the age and chemistry of its pointing? If you are writing about an animal, plant or historic personage similar researches will spring to mind. If the person is alive and undocumented, find out *by reading* all that you can about the town he comes from, his school and so on. If this is too pale a chore (the Muse pities pale chores), then study in detail some verse and prose descriptions of similar people. (After all, you are the one with the empty notebook.) Then remembering the historic dimension of your subject, and time is our nearest approach to magic, speak a description into your taperecorder, if you have one, or into empty air if you haven't. In the former case you play back and glean. In the latter you recall and make notes. You now stand as close to, or as far from, a poem as those who had full books before you started this task. And you will be richer than they are. You will have renewed your acquaintance with the printed word, with time, and with the enchantment of the trivial (which is the raw stuff of literature). Luckier still, you will have come to hear the substance of your first poem as sound, as an agitation of the air. Its pattern may already be plain before you. At least you now know how to work at your notebook and work at yourself. Take your childhood, or past life, or your environment — any subject that can be researched in archives, checked against literature, and confirmed by observation and memory — and work it layer on layer, so that each time you speak or write of it you see it in all its dimensions. Such a subject is vast enough to give you any number of second chances. You need never follow error up the same garden path.

If you have read the last page slowly, like a prescription, I wonder how many notebooks you have filled by now? The medicine has entirely beneficial side-effects. Poets, even bad ones, are generally good talkers. It is because they have given themselves time to stop their own particle of world and take a good look at it.

7.

There are games to play, little devices. They can come later. What has to be stressed now is the importance first of quest, then of calm reflection. The more you educate yourself in these twin pursuits, the more surely a seemingly trivial writing game will trigger you into activity. Writing games *are* trivial, but they won't work for fools.

We must first learn to accept that poetry can be achieved by letting the imagination play loosely over such random products of the intellect. In fact, it can be found in any casual encounter between the components of the human intelligence. The poetic intelligence is a promiscuous meeting ground, no, a cess, where our intellect, our imagination, whether vision, dream or fancy, and our senses involve themselves in a kind of selective bacteriological ferment.

To make a poem, in short, is a bit like making cheese. We cannot control the process, and yet we can predict it will turn out well if we take the trouble to get things right in the first place.

And after all of these fine words we have a confession to make. Our notebooks are still empty. Some of us did not go to the town library, or buy any books, or listen to the choir sing in Oc at S. Michel, Raissac. So how can they be full?

> You praise the firm restraint with which they write —
> I'm with you there, of course:
> They use the snaffle and the curb all right,
> But where's the bloody horse?
>
> Roy Campbell *Adamastor*

The habit must be caught even if we trivialise it. It is better to trivialise than not to practise. Certainly we shall never write a good poem if we are scared to write a bad one.

So we open our book and look quickly around us. Indoors or out, we seize quickly on something that leaps to the eye, some cup or cat or fire hydrant. Then we write, quickly again, ten one-sentence descriptions of the object. Then we write, equally quickly, ten one-sentence lies about it. Lies are intensely useful to the poet, and to the Inquisitor, because before anyone can tell a lie he has to think he knows what the truth is. Often I gaze at my vasty azimuth of falsehood and discover not only that the truth lies at its centre, but that the random ring of mendacity is in fact closer to truth than my earlier spatter of honesty. Falsehood is the inner (and sometimes the bull) to honesty's magpie or outer. In fact, as any poet knows, honesty sometimes misses the target, or the attention, altogether.

There are good lies and bad ones, of course — Burns' 'My love is like a red, red rose' against Spenser's 'Her goodly bosom like a strawberry bed . . .'

Poet's lies are called images, and how true half of them are.

I have not finished with the cup, cat or fire hydrant yet. We lazy ones are not only going to have something on paper, we may even reach to a poem sooner than the honest fillers of the book. We are now going to give ourselves a title, *Ten Views of a Cup, Cat or Fire Hydrant,* and rather more deliberately than we compiled our first two lists, taking perhaps an hour or six, we are going to enumerate ten surrealistic or bizarre or unusual descriptions of our title; and these descriptions may go on for more than a sentence or more than a line, as the case may be.

So *Ten Views of a Fire Hydrant* may become:

1. Silent letter in the South.

2. Goalpost on the wall where the gnats play rugby . . .

Save by now I am more interested in the scissors on my desk:

1. Bald ballerina with the empty eyes, the straightlegged stance and the breasts full of air.

2. My nose in a mirror behind lorgnettes.

3. Ovaries in the forbidden book.

4. Mind that has boggled as it whisked an egg . . .

I can hear you remark that this is neither original nor clever. True, but then I took my notebook to S. Michel, Raissac. I take it everywhere.

The list and the lies are more than an approach to perception, though. In the chapter on writing games I suggest a way in which your best lie can be translated into a poem. Meanwhile, wrestle with your fire hydrant and your scissors. Many people follow that road and tumble under a poem as beneath the wheels of a bus.

> Launch not beyond your Depth, but be discreet,
> And mark that Point where Sense and Dulness meet . . .
> Alexander Pope *An Essay on Criticism*

Chapter Three

The play tight, the scrums countless,
Bored and shivering out on the wing,
What sort of game are you in?

The field suddenly opens wide.
The joy of lengthening your stride.

Daniel Huws *Noth*

1.

In the same note book, the third blue one, there is a complete poem.

Among all the addle and fumble, it happened quite simply, like this.

I go quite often to that part of France, to live there and work. We all carry two landscapes in our head, one from childhood and one from manhood. Both are good to write about. Languedoc is the landscape of my adult imagination.

I was asked to contribute a poem to a birthday volume. Its recipient, Leonard Clark, in addition to being a poet of formal sensibility is a very religious man.

My hosts, on the farm where I stay, are also religious. Part of their reverence is for the rich ecology of their native landscape. They detest the Frenchman's habit of stalking across Sunday with dog and gun and killing everything that moves.

I had already written one poem about *La Chasse*. It had turned itself into a political lament for the victims of the wine ambush in the Corbières. I was ready for something with a more religious, and ecological, focus.

I used to hunt as a youth, so I knew the psychology of slaughter. In preparation for the earlier poem, pretty random preparation at that, I had read some of the literature of hunting, particularly any writings that dealt with the philosophy of the huntsman. I paid special attention to hunter philosophies as they could be found embodied in the beliefs of primitive peoples.

17

Against this I had the background of a Western Christo-Judaic culture.

So if the poem was there, I was prepared for it. Time was of the essence. I could not let the poem lead me to its lair and teach me a form. I had to have a hutch for it, something simple, received and durable. The ballad (or hymn) was the obvious choice. I proposed it to the poem and the poem stepped into it.

GUNSMEN

Blueskinned with good morning
gunsmen front the breeze,
roll up rabbit carpets,
sieve blood through cut glass trees

and all day long they dandle
the dead meat in their smile.
I smell them. They go walking
their death's concentric mile.

No ghost goes on before them;
no thing stays live behind,
no fin, no fluff, no feather
in the long smear of their mind.

Save One who walks there lonely
and both ways of the breeze
rolls up no rabbit carpets
nor sieves the blood of trees:

That Gunsman dreams of nothing,
no lightnings leave his head;
his flesh glares down no shadow,
he roves on weightless tread.

Butterflies fumble through him,
Birds unwise his hair
and cobwebs blind his barrel
to nest and set and lair:

and, gunsmen, he kills nothing
but gives the dead flesh back,
walking the broken pastures
with tomorrow in his sack.

The immediate problem here was not the form — I chose one more or less ready made, one that I could listen to before I wrote. The challenge was that the form was a rhyming one. So however I shaped the experience within and beyond the succession of stanzas, I still had to make rhyme work for me.

Rhyme is a terrible trap. For example, after I typed the Graves quotation above, I jotted in my notebook (perhaps punning on *Graves?*): *The truth digs all our coffins.*

Without pausing to ask myself just what such a line might mean, I find it pointing me towards an epigram. When I was fifteen I would have looked immediately for a hard rhyme for 'coffins'; and if 'boffins' had presented itself (there isn't much else) I should have accepted it as gratefully as a lettuce sandwich.

As a guzzler of the obvious I should have forgotten that a rhyme must do the following things.

It must present the reader with a word which is intellectually and aesthetically appropriate to the whole poem or its place in the poem.

It must not call attention to itself by being obtrusive and discordant.

Most important, it must never appear to lead the meaning of a line. Nor must it seem to predetermine the assonance and general structure of the verse in which it occurs. To find a rhyme is to begin our troubles, not end them.

A rhymster is like a conjuror. His sleight must be to keep the attention of his readers elsewhere. He does this by stress, by syntax, by enjambment, and the sheer force of self-preservation.

2.

Nonetheless, a good new rhyme can startle continents. When Auden rhymed 'islands' and 'silence', he launched a thousand imitators into activity, so much so that they overlooked Eliot's prior claim on the words.

When we must rhyme, we should not use a rhyming dictionary but our intelligence, and strive to make it total.

Never mind what the computer says, there are not that many

true rhymes in a fine consonantal language like English. Half rhymes such as Eliot's and Auden's are nearly always the product of outrageous wit. A cliché rhyme (most rhymes *are* clichés) can be carried by the overall shape of the line, and by its sense if we give its sense space in which to work. Fortunately most English stanzas are extraordinarily spacious, so much so that our ideas are in danger of rattling about in them.

> If man is divine, language is his divinity.
> John Moat *A Standard of Verse*

Only a very few poems come easily. For some poets, none. By keeping a notebook, carrying writing materials (not necessarily the same thing), by reading other poets, by broadening our interest and observation and thus increasing our sense of *self* in the world, we put ourselves in the way of attracting such a poem. I wish you many of them.

The fact is, though, that the developing itch to write a poem is very rarely a desire to write *this* poem. To be a poet is now our choice. We exercise our will upon our choice by trying to write *a* poem, that is all. *I want to write a poem: I have no poem to write* — this is an expression of one of life's ironies, not your own inadequacy. To be a poet is like being on the verge of love without finding anyone to love. Mature, practised poets have exactly the same feeling, the old fatuous ache. Without it they would not begin. It is just that they know where the pick-ups are.

If you do glimpse a poem, even if you cannot 'listen' to it, then of course it is good to attempt a draft if there is a draft to attempt. Many is the man, woman, dog or tax inspector from Porlock who will stop this moment's clarity reaching paper if you lack 'world enough (writing materials) and time (a little patience)' to inscribe it there.

Perhaps there is no clear vision, just a line, a phrase, an image, an agitation of the soul or bowel. Set down what you have, whether from soul or bowel, and leave it. Brood upon it. Brood upon it and forget it. Good poets forget endlessly. Oblivion opens the mind. If you have a good filing system, or even a well-kept notebook called Charles Armitage Brown, it will return to re-inspire you, perhaps to another line, phrase, image, or agitation of the soul or bowel.

Most of us won't glimpse a poem. Such is our fortunate tragedy.

If you are growing impatient, skip a few pages and try one of those writing exercises. Or simply give up.

You will like yourself better if you go somewhere quiet in the house, lay out your paper, and sit comfortably to wait for your poem.

Of course, it won't come at once, so you must do something to help it reveal itself.

If your notebook fails you, there are these two choices.

Either empty your mind completely and wait for the ideas to rise (it sounds very fey, but then it is fey, scrattling about for a poem).

Or deliberately summon ideas by reviewing all of the things in your life that interest you (your notebook should be making this a reflex process by now): music, hill-walking, being alone, car engines, tasting wine, it does not matter what — then concentrate on the one that brings the biggest buzz, the most detailed itch. Then lay it out piecemeal. You will certainly have the components of a poem or some other highly charged writing. If you have a small study space, you may want to help the process by chasing the idea through books. The word is a powerful catalyst for the word. But I cannot emphasise too strongly the energy to be gained by simply emptying the mind. If you can cancel things out for just a few seconds then your environment will rearrange itself in a new order. You will be able to see it with a fresh eye. Till now you have been collecting yourself. Now you are about to review and use yourself.

This may seem nothing, but you have nothing else.

21

Solitude for the moment is important. If you cannot be alone or concentrate at home then go for a walk. Walking itself, as Wordsworth, Hazlitt, Dickens knew, is a great churner of the brain. Take your notebook with you and find somewhere quiet, or withdrawn, outside. If you are a country dweller this will be easy; but in towns I have found parks, seats, embankments, anonymous bars, the soft underbellies of bridges. We do not need to be alone to find solitude. If something on our walk takes enough of our attention — the train's passing flaking dust from an iron bridge, an old person feeding birds in the park — then we can easily withdraw into the necessary thought.

If solitude is impossible, then don't forget the local library. There is a tremendous concentration of calm in a good library. But better, far better, recharge your home. If your normal workplace, where you do your accounts or write your chess correspondence, seems alien to poetry, try somewhere else. Try your workshed or your spare bedroom. Better still, use the kitchen table. In a good house all the best things happen in the kitchen. My writing has often been done alone in the kitchen in the peevish but sullenly relaxed small hours with soups bubbling away on the stove.

Probably you have never achieved good writing before, at school say, because the environment has been so psychically antiseptic that it has deadened the bug of invention. There is nothing like working under and over and round a meal eaten all by yourself when the dull world is asleep. If you are forced to seek solitude at antisocial hours, then make solitude a festival. Mozart liked to compose in the kitchen among the wreckage of a private feast, and he was not alone in refusing to suppose that inspiration should be uncomfortable.

Then I am a well-fleshed cycloid, among poets most amiably pyknyk. I must not overlook the fact that discomfort, whether of sleet or heat, sharpens some people's minds, witness the fondness of the Prophets for the Wilderness.

All this and not a note struck?

I sense even now a most costive striving.

5.

Any old love affair serves to bring me out in a sonnet.
Michael Baldwin

22

We do not merely wait with our pens aimed at silence. What sort of beast is this poem we are hunting? We can ask ourselves that, and we can determine to have a profound effect on it in advance of its leaping from the shadows, whether it springs from our own or God's or the flint's head.

Our images, our lies and our truths, are already there on its pelt. Everything we have done so far has seen to that.

Our images and perhaps a few poets' else.

Our research lies heavy in its bowels. Its loins bristle with our high intent.

We cannot 'hear' it yet, we do not know its tune; but we can put ourself in the way of hearing it.

Our poem, whatever it is, must move; and if it moves, then clearly it must follow a path, the path of form in a rhetorical sense, and of form in an aesthetic sense.

Often when I shake my head and try to listen to my poem in advance, I have to remind myself of this simple literary fact. When Eliot spoke of a poem needing to have at least the virtues of good prose, he was not talking merely of grammar and sense, nor even of style. He meant, above everything else, that it should not be dull. In the broadest sense he meant that it should move and narrate its meaning.

Given that our poem should move, and that once it moves we shall be able to listen to it move towards form, we should be able to bring it at least half way out of its lair.

Even if we do not have a subject, we should be able to take one from our notebook, cluster our research and observation about it, then ask ourself how it will move.

That dull brick wall, say, the one that has withstood so many editions of the ordnance survey. Is it to settle into the years an oblong quatrain at the time, to the tramp of labourers' boots, or is it to undulate across the windy rhythms of the hills until the landscape explodes or breaks? It may still do so in quatrains, of course — there is more to form than stanzas — but they will be different quatrains, just as the form will be different. Surely you can *listen* to your poem now, hear its bone-cracking lurch into form? Surely it is beginning to move?

No poet can hope to understand the nature of poetry unless he has had a vision of the Naked King crucified to the lopped oak, and watched the dancers ... stamping out the measure of the dance ...
Robert Graves *The White Goddess*

Yes, the poem will move all right. If only movement were the end of it.

6.

I took my binoculars ten miles beyond Raissac and went to watch the boar hunt. I also took two unpleasant encounters with wild boar, one in an enclosure on Cleve Hill and one with a sanglier in the nearby pines.

The following day the poem began to write itself quite easily; but in rereading it until it moves into trouble I have to remind myself that although very close to the boar and the poem I wrote them not with pen or gun but with binoculars. Binoculars take you very close indeed, of course, and I was close enough already; but binoculars take you close to everything quite equally. So does memory and dream.

Perhaps the poem would become different if I could call it *Memory* or *Dream* or, better, *Poem Through Binoculars*. But I went to hunt a wild boar so I called it simply *Sanglier*.

I also went to hunt a poem, and this confuses the outcome as well.

> The Boar squealed out,
> Dogsize, no — bigger,
> The Boar came squeaking out
> Growing bigger as it ran than the bush that had hidden it,
> Growing bigger as it came than its whole back of bush.
> Four barrels merely spotted it,
> Combing corrugations in its hang-mail of mud,
>   its hair wall of mud
> Which was bristling with bone.
>
> Somebody ran.
>
> Someone, all man, the Mayor or the Grandson of the Mayor
> Hit it full on,
> Firing both barrels to deflect its open bite,
>
> Reddening its nose
>   doing nothing else
> By so much as a squeal
>
>   than the girl in the meadow picking flowers
>
> Than myself firing straight at a poem.

24

> 'Tis hard to say, if greater Want of Skill
> Appear in Writing or in Judging ill;
> But, of the two, less dang'rous is th'Offence,
> To tire our Patience, than mis-lead our Sense:
>   Alexander Pope *Essay on Criticism*

The girl is there because she was there, and because Breughel would have put her there. Neither reason is good enough.

The last line is there because the poem ought to end someway. Even though I have predisposed you to think that poetry-hunting is what the poem is about, I still think that the line, and the reasoning behind it, do not work.

What I have here is no more than a first draft. I have, of course, drafted it several times before reaching this 'first draft'. I notice from my notebook that 'hang-mail' and 'hair-wall' began as alternatives, and that I kept them because I had been experimenting with that kind of repetitive verse movement.

That being said, there were repetitions lower down that I cut out. The third from last line began as 'Not so much as by a squeal,' then lost its first word, then inverted towards its more usual (though less forceful?) final syntax.

The second from last line began as 'Doing no more than the girl in the meadow picking flowers', which is lumpy but which would certainly have reinforced a more repetitive rhetoric.

The last line was originally six lines long. I am so ashamed of the general drift of the meaning in that part of the poem that I do not propose to let you gloat over the variorum text. I am, in fact, working on another last line which is also six lines long and makes another point entirely; and I may find I am equally ashamed of that.

So *Sanglier* or *Poem through Binoculars*, or whatever the title is, is an unfinished poem. If you are at a loose end you could consider finishing it, or restarting it in another form. To do this with another poet's work, generally a nineteenth century poet, is one of my writing exercises.

That was not my reason for parading this draft, though. The reason is that here is a poem that has been 'heard', that has been encouraged to leap into the light and declare its form.

Or half leap. It is only half way out of its lair, and consequently the larger, less formal problems of form — how does it end? what does it move towards? — remain unsolved.

25

Every poem, whether it is our first or our thousandth, must not only solve itself, but solve itself in relation to the poet's overall purpose which connects with ourself and literature at large.

We must learn from our poems. We must learn not only to give them a pelt, and a stomach and loins, and to discover their movement, but to look for their heads.

We must concentrate on their heads and make sure they have some brains in them.

The heart is in ourself.

> When it comes to the meaning of anything, even the simplest word, then you must pause. Because there are two great categories of meaning, forever separate. There is mob-meaning, and there is individual meaning.
>
> D. H. Lawrence *Pornography and Obscenity*

7.

No need to worry that our poem lacks an end and possibly a beginning. We need only to catch the beast by the tail. Extracting him from the hole takes no more than patience and hard work. And a little luck.

It is a matter of choice and instinct whether we continue the extraction or work with what we have got. After all, the beast is not precisely known to us, the conceit will not stretch for ever and it is just possible that when we have brushed the mud from what we can see of it, we shall find that the rest is not length of sinew and an endless serpentine tail, but needless dirt and shadow. Instinct then. We know if there is more to find.

The real problem for us — and it is a matter of middle as well as end and beginning — is why write the poem in the first place?

It is the problem I face at that poem's end. In spite of a million protestations of high endeavour it cannot always be faced at the beginning. To the question *what will this poem be about?* we can often only answer *this poem will be about this poem* and add *when this poem knows what it will be.* Criticism cannot always precede or even accompany creation. Judgment, even the judgment of genius, needs time. Our thoughts no less than our lines have to be sat over. We write, in other words, in order to write.

Or some of us do.

26

Eliot absolves again. The mistake, he says, is not necessarily in writing but in publishing. The thwart disnatured beast is our own and for our eyes only until we are bold or brash or rash enough to lead it into the show ring.

Whether we publicise our bestiary or lock all our monsters in a private zoo, we must find the will to go on hunting.

Artistic ego is the usual inspiration; and it is dangerously similar to Fame the Spur.

Artistic ego, the feeling *this must be right because I have done my best with it,* is all very well as far as it goes. I shall suggest some ways past it later.

The trouble is that it overbears criticism and not merely self-criticism but criticism of the world.

Our first task is nonetheless to overbear the world.

> The abyss is not yet filled to overflowing. It is full only to the rim.
>
> *The Book of Changes*

Of course our early work will be presumptuous and derivative; and our later best endeavours be no better than other poets' and possibly not very different.

It is in the nature of literature to be full of echoes. It is bound to be because it is full of words.

The real test of a poem is not *does it duplicate?*

The real test of a poem is *is it alive?*

Chapter Four

By day I adhered to my desk, and at night, a pale student, I consumed the midnight oil. You should have seen me — you *should*. I leaned to the right. I leaned to the left. I sat forward. I sat backward. I sat *tête baissée* (as they have it in the Kickapoo), bowing my head close to the alabaster page. And, through all, I *wrote*. Through joy and through sorrow I — *wrote*. Through hunger and through thirst I — *wrote*. Through good report and through ill report I — *wrote*. Through sunshine and through moonshine I — *wrote*. *What* I wrote it is unnecessary to say. The *style*! — that was the thing. I caught it from Fatquack.

Edgar Allan Poe *The Literary Life of Thingum Bob, Esq.*

1.

'The poet's medium,' says C. Day-Lewis, 'is words.' It is difficult to fault such a profundity — I wish Poe were at my elbow to try — but the feeling remains that he might just as well say 'ink' or 'bitumen' or 'subterranean wind'.

Now we have our poem beginning to grunt and stir, we have to groom it, of course. I am with him there. Words have to be right in themselves, and not merely as they curl or cluster with others.

But they do curl and cluster with others, so it might be better to say that they have to be right one by one as well as two by two.

There are three solutions to this problem of grooming:

We have to read other poets avidly and critically.

We have to reread our own poems no less avidly and no less critically, and we have to keep an anxious eye cocked towards the experience they claim to spring from.

This is already a trifocal occupation, with hints of the pineal, but we can simplify it a little.

If we turn towards poets dead and gone, we can observe their problems rather more in the round than we can see our own. Many of them moreover have been subjected to comparative textual scrutiny by generations of scholars, and the results have been collated and published. We are thus able to compare draft with draft and to reflect that it will be wise to drop as many as we can of our own inside a dustbin or, if we become famous, a furnace.

With energy, bus-trips to libraries and so on, we can play this game at quite a high level. We can even victimise some of our more foolish or impoverished contemporaries if we are prepared to buy aeroplane tickets to and around America.

But in truth, most major writers exist in some reasonably accessible variorum edition or other. When they do not, the serial editions such as *Oxford Standard Authors,* include their unfinished particles, and because these are incomplete there is usually more than one version of them. This is especially true of the Romantics, who were liberal pliers of the pen.

Alternative, rather than variorum, editions of Wordsworth are easy to come by — *The Prelude* is commonly printed in two versions, the 1805 and 1850; and it is interesting to view a great author at the height of two different sorts of power. School editions of Wordsworth generally include a very full variorum (as do school editions of nearly everyone else) in those textual footnotes we became so used to ignoring at school. We must now start to take notice of them. I harp on Wordsworth (as I say, nearly *all* school editions or college editions offer equally rich pickings over an entire range of authors) because with the arguable exception of *The Prelude* editions, his powers noticeably decline and many of his revisions are retrograde. This is not something to savour but to experience with him. Wordsworth, for all his foibles, was forging a style in the teeth of more recent tradition, a tradition which his genius had to attempt to cancel in himself. As he grew older and his genius declined the tradition that his youth despised began to take him over again. To read Wordsworth sympathetically is one of life's great adventures anyway, because what he does best seems almost to be achieved *beyond* style (the reason he fares so badly with some modern textual critics, but not — I hope — with his fellow poets). But *everything* he does, good or bad, is done on the very frontiers of style; and that is where we are now.

There are different signposts and different maps, but that is where we are or where we must seek to place ourselves.

Bound with cords and ropes,
Shut in between thorn-hedged prison walls:
For three years one does not find the way.
                                    The Book of Changes

Easier to concentrate our minds on something at a more aloof distance from ourselves. Here is Pope, more than a little ill but toiling at his translation of the *Iliad*.

He scribbles on many ill-assorted scraps of paper, bills, letters, wrappers and so on — he even bundles up a gift of cherries in one, and has to ask for it back — and he corrects ceaselessly.

Impossible to indicate the sequence of correction by typographic means, still less the process of his mind. So here is everything he wrote on one such scrap, followed by the corrected passage as it is printed in the *World's Classics* edition. We can see at once that his concerns went far beyond the mere ordering of couplets. They are very much to do with words one by one and two by two.

Dredful he shouts: from earth a stone he rends took
And rushed on Teucer with the lifted rock
And with the lifted rock on Teucer bends.
Already the chief alredy bent strained the forceful yew
The shaft alredy to his shoulder drew
The feather in his hand, now just winged for flight
Just touched where the neck and hollow chest unite
An easy path to death there fiercely thrown on the channel bone
A mortal part. There on the channel bone
A mortal part on that juncture thrown
The Trojan chief discharged the ponderous stone,
The sounding bowstring bursts before beneath the blow,
And his numbed hand forsakes the his useless bow.
He falls. But Ajax his broad shield displayed,
And guards screened his brother with his its mighty shade;
Mecistheus then, and great Alastor Till great Alastor Mecistheus
    bore
The groaning warrior to the sea-beat shore.
The battered warrior groaning to the shore.

I have not reproduced any of Pope's abbreviations or elisions, as the eye has enough to contend with, nor his spellings save *already/alredy* where he is inconsistent, and *dredful* since it bears on *already*.

This is what remains after the smelting:

Dreadful he shouts: from earth a stone he took,
And rush'd on Teucer with the lifted rock.

The youth already strain'd the forceful yew;
The shaft already to his shoulder drew;
The feather in his hand, just wing'd for flight,
Touch'd where the neck and hollow chest unite;
There, where the juncture knits the channel bone,
The furious chief discharged the craggy stone:
The bow-string burst beneath the ponderous blow,
And his numb'd hand dismissed his useless bow.
He fell: but Ajax his broad shield display'd,
And screen'd his brother with the mighty shade;
Till great Alastor, and Mecistheus, bore
The batter'd archer groaning to the shore.

The style is elevated but not ornate. The words need to be appropriate to the subject and to the way the poet deals with it. Pope is making a translation from a primary heroic epic, and can be supposed to be at some distance from the Homeric canon, however enthusiastically he views it. What he gives us is the definitive Augustan *Iliad*.

In many ways we are as far from the Augustans as they are from Homer. So we can view Pope's revisions with considerable detachment, more so than Wilfred Owen's, say, or Eliot's in *The Waste Land* (another accessible text), much more than our own. We can see his scale of preferences. He wishes his words to please the ear, to be intellectually, aurally and imaginatively at ease with one another, and — as we said above — to be appropriate to the subject.

You may write about micro-chips, micro-waves, radar, sonar, quasars, pulsars, black holes, intergalactic travel and computer banks. Our concerns include nuclear war, urban encroachment and decay, and world starvation; and yet we must still find words which are appropriate to our subject and purpose, words which are not mutually offensive, and words which please, or at least consider, the ear.

Whether a poem is written in stanzas or one of the so-called 'free' or 'new' forms, its clusters of words must obey and develop a double ordering. It is this ordering, much more than the interior narrative or the exterior shape, that will keep it moving ahead and prevent it being dull. Hypnotic it may be, but never dull. The word-clusters must develop in the ear throughout the poem, and their meanings must develop in the imagination, that inner eye. Without that twin accord, poetry will never happen. In this sense, and only in this perhaps, a poem is like a piece of music. It can last for as long as it can extend its original proposition.

Our task for the moment is to make it last at all. Consider this extract from Hopkin's *The Wreck Of The Deutschland:*

On Saturday sailed from Bremen,
American-outward-bound,
Take settler and seaman, tell men with women,
Two hundred souls in the round —
O Father, not under thy feathers nor ever as guessing
The goal was a shoal, of a fourth the doom to be drowned;
Yet did the dark side of the bay of thy blessing
Not vault them, the millions of rounds of thy mercy not reeve
    even them in?

Into the snow she sweeps,
Hurling the haven behind,
The Deutschland, on Sunday; and so the sky keeps
For the infinite air is unkind,
And the sea flint-flake, black-backed in the regular blow,
Sitting Eastnortheast, in cursed quarter, the wind;
Wiry and white-fiery and whirlwind swivelled snow
Spins in the widow-making unchilding unfathering deeps.

Then without taking too much of a breath — I know you are chewing it pip and rind, like a poet — follow it with these stanzas from Auden's *On This Island:*

Here at the small field's ending pause
When the chalk wall falls to the foam and its tall ledges
Oppose the pluck
And knock of the tide,
And the shingle scrambles after the sucking surf,
And the gull lodges
A moment on its sheer side.

Far off like floating seeds the ships
Diverge on urgent voluntary errands,
And the full view
Indeed may enter
And move in memory as now these clouds do,
That pass the harbour mirror
And all the summer through the water saunter.

In general, ear and eye relationships are less intrusive in Auden's poetry, but they are very strong in the passage I have quoted, and he certainly has Hopkins very much in mind. There are devices and echoes here that are not to be found in the Anglo-Saxon and

Middle English poetry they both so much admired. Some critics find too much thrust in this style, but no one disputes the fact that it is deliberate and self-aware.

Hopkins, and the Auden of this poem, offer us extreme, almost coagulated examples of the twin qualities I wish to stress. I believe that the greatest artist uses a lighter brush and thins his paint rather more. Yet a beginner — and we are always beginning and rebeginning — should start heavy and strong. Exercises should be heavy and strong. Writing games should be heavy and strong. So should limbers and warm-ups. We should always insist on reminding ourselves what we are about: a good poem must at the very least be good rhetoric. If we get the colour right we can always thin out the lumps.

> A God can do it. But can a man expect
> to penetrate the narrow lyre and follow?
> His sense is discord. Temples for Apollo
> are not found where two heart-ways intersect.
>
> For song, as taught by you, is not desire,
> not wooing of something finally attained;
> song is existence . . .
>
> Rilke *Sonnets to Orpheus III*,
> translated by J. B. Leishman

3.

Whether or not our poetry should speak in heightened tones or in the 'language of ordinary men' is for us to decide. There are no laws, though many fools try to make them. But high or low, fleshy or wiry, we should always write without padding or embellishment. If our style is talkative, we must keep it away from chatty vulgarity. If it is elevated, we must remember that gas expands with altitude. There is nothing worse than pomposity yawing and swelling till it loses its last molecule in the vacuum. We must remember, too, that all styles have their clichés, those old ladies' props that hold up the billowing line of verse. Our poetry must not lean on them. They are never the carved and polished hardwood they seem to be, but flabby as expanded polystyrene. Besides, a cliché by definition belongs to all men. Our poem must be our own.

We must work simply, directly and accurately. Hemingway has

a good phrase, although he and others have overworked it. He speaks of a piece of writing (or a pass in the bull-ring) as being achieved 'without faking'. We must copy those words and pin them away in the mind.

Nine tenths of the people who set out to write poetry experience a kind of mauve fog in the brain. Or it may be red fog or white fog or dun fog. I only know it is fog, and I know it because they produce such foggy words. Strange archaisms appear, shapes loom and gloom and beckon, but no meaning follows. Their ordinary common sense as civil servants, nurses, traffic wardens, bank managers — whatever they are — seems to desert them. Gone are their terse business sentences, their terser prescriptions and summonses, because they are writing poetry with a penful of fog.

If this keeps on happening, a bad case of lingering fog, or if we find ourselves costive with archaisms, or images that will not draw together and explode in the brain, it is worth writing some of our poems out as prose. You can't do that to a good poem? Not quite true. A good poem always leaves something of itself in prose, and its rhetoric will thin and straighten. But bad poems, poems suffering from fog, defy paraphrase.

The fog may only be patchy, of course. A lot of fog hangs over poetry, and some of it is good poetry. Later I want to talk about the role of the writing circle, or of family and friends, when we consider the poet's audience. For the moment I should just like to say that if we are unsure of a poem we should make use of its first audience, its private audience, by asking the reader or listener to tell us what it is about. This is often more rewarding, and less socially uncomfortable, than asking people what they think of it. A simple observation from beyond the buzz of our own skull may point us in a fresh direction and show the way to a new start.

He has committed an *ignoratio elenchi* — that is he has understood the words of your proposition but not the idea. The man was *a fool*, you see. Some poor fellow whom you addressed while choking with that chicken bone . . .
Edgar Allan Poe *How To Write A Blackwood Article*

There is, I confess, something rather nasty underlying this chapter,
something that gnaws and niggles and refuses to go away. It is this:
in talking about eye and ear and appropriate language we are only
paying lip-service to rhetoric, and if we only pay lip-service to
rhetoric we only pay lip-service to poetry. Form is an abstract
proposition until we confront some of its more mundane structures,
such as metre and stanza. Even if we think of so-called free form
we had better reduce it to something we can see. It is now, in short,
that I must direct the beginner (and myself) towards the second
half of this book, not for his inspection but for his consideration
and practice. Poetry is surely going wrong. Never have so many of
us been so good (I do hope history will agree); but very few of us
will prove to be that good (I am sure I can hear history begin to
stretch her lips in approval).

Let us bring Doctor Johnson in at once, and attach his deposition
to Eliot's on Sweeney and Pound's on *Mauberley*.

> *Blank verse,* said an ingenious critick, *seems to* be verse
> only to the eye.
>   Poetry may subsist without rhyme, but English poetry
> will not often please; nor can rhyme ever be safely spared
> but where the subject is able to support itself . . . I cannot
> prevail upon myself to wish that Milton had been a rhymer;
> for I cannot wish his work to be other than it is; yet like
> other heroes, he is to be admired rather than imitated. He
> that thinks himself capable of astonishing, may write blank
> verse; but those that hope only to please, must
> condescend to rhyme.
>   Samuel Johnson *Lives of the Poets*

Mutatis mutandis, of course, dear Doctor. Do we hope to please,
or do we think ourselves capable of astonishing? So many of us?
Never has imagination been so fertile and free. Of that we can be
clear. I have an awful feeling, though, that from the viewpoint of
2001 my imagination will smell a bit like your imagination, and
both of them like the dustman's.

Here is a poem that many of us will recognise, because we have
at some time or other tried to write it. I have never managed to

write it this well, so I have not published it. Linda Thompson has.
It is very pleasing, and twenty like it would make an amiable book.

NOW THE BIRDS HAVE GONE

As
two tooth-throb planes
scrape-skin their own clouds,
an old man
looks up at the sky,
but it doesn't seem to know him —
perhaps there have been changes
at the top —
it was a long time ago.

A long time ago
when the first light
tingled and stretched
with the dawn,
when the birds,
swift wisps in the air,
brought the morning
on honey and lemon streamers,
everything whistling and itching
on fine-feathered branches,
the sky smiling the lyric,
the birds the tune.

The old man
looks down at the ground,
but it does not stir,
is dark and silent,
bored and listless,
having nothing
to torment it
and tickle its ribs,
to peck holes in it,
nothing to complain about
anymore
now the birds have gone.

Now the birds have gone
the actress has forsaken her diamonds
and wears a priceless feather in her cap,
an exhibition of starling's eggs
and droppings
draws five-mile queues
outside the British Museum,
an artist
draws his impression
of wings and summers.

The old man
stops the world,
brings out the flaking past,
rubs it in his palms
and fills his head.

'A blackbird at my window'

he speaks a child-dream touch.

A woman shopper turns and stares
at the prehistoric mammal
who talks of
nothing on earth.

This is an expansive poem on a huge subject. Although it is to do
with a sombre vision it has a Liverpudlian lyricism that reminds me
of Henri, Patten and McGough. It also has something of their
perkiness, their early reluctance to deepen a theme. It pleases (but
is it *meant* to please? And if it is, should it? Or should it seek to
touch us with awe?) It does not astonish us, though, as Hughes,
say, or Atwood astonish — to name two major exponents of the
nearly free.

It is not meant to astonish, surely?

I am sure it is not. But if it is not, then I believe with Johnson
that such a poem should pay more attention to the details of form,
the more so since the poet gets so many of the larger things right.

It may seem a peculiarly American obsession, and it may appear
to belong to the structured writing course rather than to the real
life of the imagination, but I believe we should pay a great deal of
attention to form. English Literature as a discipline, particularly as
it is taught in English universities, has nothing to do with creativity
or fostering the creative process. There is no corner of any syllabus
that even bothers to examine, let alone encourage, such a thing.

The philosophy is that if it cannot be measured then it cannot be examined. If it cannot be examined it cannot be taught. Consequentially English Literature ignores writers and writers ignore it. I cannot think of a more saddening or wasteful divorce. The more so since so many of us are deliberately and insolently ignorant about the well-springs of our tradition and the deserts they might irrigate for us. It is fair both ends on, of course. If our own mental processes are scruffy enough to confuse Literature with Eng. Lit., and blame one for the shortcomings of the other, we can hardly be surprised if exponents of either banish our concerns to Sociology, Psychology or the recently developed dustbin of Contemporary Linguistics.

The exile can be comfortable for the poet, and in many cases it is self-sought. To take the narrower point merely, to work in metre, rhyme, stanza, even unrhymed syllabics, is to work with pain. It is also to work with something that can be formally measured and assessed, at least to a degree.

In one of his early poems Graves tells us that poets can be sorted by shape and size as easily as apples — 'Any honest wife could sort them out . . .' I sometimes believe that this is why so many of us operate beyond the limit of normal market standards. The only test we can apply to ourselves is to return to apple-growing from time to time, and make sure that we produce good apples.

Graves is an uneasy writer with an uneasy reputation; he is rejected by writers and scholars about equally, though of course not universally, and this is because his writing and his scholarship have in large measure been devoted to the history and diagnosis of the creative process.

If method is important, then so is its history. The poet learned intricate numbers and with them wove webs with which to snare the Muse, if he came from a hunting community. And more latterly, he built trellises of light on which the feathered particles could perch and sing. Sometimes, as with the Celtic schools, he served an apprenticeship which had a professed psychic, even occult, dimension. At the least he had to acquire secret knowledge, to be able to speak of the sacred trees by their magic names and make his deductions from such information much as an Australian Aborigine learns his waterholes by reference to a notched bark which defies cartographic interpretation. It may be that all of this is no more than work and pain, and that we should abhor the latter just as we do the ritual circumcision of boys or the tribal skin-marking of girls. Not, though, the work; for there, surely, at the end of it is the power, the power of adult tribalism, and in the case of the fledged poet the gift of Tongue, alike in importance to the Mage's or Apostle's Gift of Tongues. Yes, perhaps only work was involved, but it was dedicated tortuous stuff and subject to many rebuffs and frustrations, and at the end of it was the admission to the mystery, that convenient medieval word which embraces both trade and miracle.

So I find it odd when I meet contemporary poets whose work is always 'free', who have never found it necessary at some point in their development to play with some, or all, of the stricter forms mentioned at the back of this book. In the case of Linda Thompson and young writers like her, it strikes me as more sad than odd; and in the case of the beginner, impertinent.

Still a devotee of the Muse, a preacher of the free, a convert to the religion of inspiration? Yes, indeed. Poetry is the art of faith, not of doubt. But faith needs good works to build upon.

> I think for the young poet, the writing poet, it is not quite so frightening to go to university in America as it is in England.
>
> Sylvia Plath *The Poet Speaks*

Chapter Five

'To pen an Ode upon the "Oil-of-Bob"
Is all sorts of a job.
                    (signed) SNOB.'

To be sure this composition was of no very great length, — but I
'have yet to learn', as they say in the *Edinburgh Review,* that the
mere extent of a literary work has anything to do with its merit.
As for the *Quarterly* cant about 'sustained effort' . . .

Edgar Allan Poe *The Literary Life of*
Thingum Bob, Esq.

1.

The notebooks are still empty, the typing paper virgin as snow.
Still, we cannot research our interior waste land for ever, nor do
we always have the energy to turn to the back of the book and play
at *villanelles, ballades,* and *pantoums* till we have proved
conclusively that Baldwin (and Doctor Johnson) are wrong.

So here are my writing games, warm-ups, limbers, call them
what you will, the morning-after substitutes for hard work; but
nonetheless all quite capable of calling up the Muse.

Extended Lies

You already have your ten lies, whether surreal, truly mendacious
or merely metaphor. Pick the one that seems most capable of
development, then add two more lies to it that continue its meaning
without returning you to artistic truth.

So, if you wrote:

The stars are little tintacks

you can add:

They hold up night's curtain
Then the sun comes and tears it

What a pleasing idea to drown in a sherry glass. Then, because easy is not lazy, you can revise it, making it a continuous sentence, or what ever flows freely and makes the point best:

> The stars are little tintacks
> Holding (pinning? nailing?) night's curtain
> Till the sun (dawn? day? daylight?) tears it . . .

Then, if your interest quickens, you can turn it into a haiku.

Then you can write a whole sequence of three line lies. Question to prompt your own parallels: why 'little tintacks'? why 'tintacks'? why 'curtain' and not, say, 'blanket'? The mind begins its spirals.

Syllabics

This is a thoroughly respectable form, or *approach* rather, with a good Graeco-Roman pedigree. You can, if you like, combine rhymes or 'backwords' (see later) with this form. The beauty of the whole thing is that although this way of making poetry is full of pain, you, rather than a textbook of prosody, determine the shape of the torture.

Method: write down an extended sentence that can be arbitrarily distributed over four to six lines. It can be your sentence or someone else's, metric or not. If you *hope* to turn it into a poem, *your* poem, then it will need to be highly charged from your wit or your notebook:

> The tar-stepping horse
> With invisible eyes
> Draws a rag-and-bone cart and a rag-and-bone carter
> To the distant junction
> Where he breathes out cobwebs

Then you count the number of syllables (not stresses) in each line (I make it five, six, thirteen, six, six) and develop the movement of the idea through several more verses by writing sentences of exactly the same syllabic length as your first one, and so arranged that they can be distributed into similar line-lengths (five, six, thirteen, six, six — or whatever your pattern is), without breaking words on the enjambment.

That is if you lack energy, and I know you don't. The *more teasing way* is to notate your opening stanza so that you know how many syllables there are in each word in every line (you may count compounds as composites or separates), something like:

    1, 3, 1
    1, 4, 1
    1, 1, 3, 1, 1, 1, 3, 2
    1, 1, 2, 2
    1, 1, 1, 1, 2

To match this pattern *word by word* instead of line by line through several more stanzas is a substantial challenge, but it encourages a much more muscular rhythm. In fact, you are inventing a metre for yourself. Caution: be wary of single-syllables no less than very long words. Witness my doodle below, based on a sentence overfull of monosyllables.

> The meticulous boxer
> With the high-held hands
> And elastic stance
> Shoots out a left then a left, then a right.
>
> He exaggerates gestures,
> Stomps toe-to-toe with
> His clumsier, square-
> -styled jab-and-jab, left-and-right hand foe
>
> Who insistently flurries
> Axe-like broad-hammed thumps
> Through simpering air
> Left and right, miss, jab and jab, miss . . . miss . . . miss
>
> Till frustratedly seeking
> The ropes he lies back
> On electric strands
> Live with pain, racks breath and waits for the bell.

It reads like an exercise, of course; but some poets, Herbert Read, George MacBeth, Ted Walker have learned to ease themselves into the challenge so that their work moves sweetly; and, of course, they allow themselves variants on the initial ground rules.

Shapes

This is a much more relaxed way to play with syllabics. We think of a shape, such as an hourglass or a diamond, then build it in words by adding to, or subtracting from, a line-length a syllable at

42

a time. The challenge, small enough but good for before breakfast, is to choose a subject which suits the shape:

LADY IN AN OLD-FASHIONED DRESS

Old-fashioned   hourglass lady
In your   hourglass dress
With the wide shoulders
Tapering seams
And thumb-thick
Slender
Waist,
I   love
Your gliding
Delicate steps,
Your gravely   planted
Yet   fragile   silhouette,
Old-fashioned   hourglass lady.

The shape is syllabic, not visual, so it really exists in the head. You can give yourself toothache (the subject of many a poem) by trying to make it work on the typewriter.

ROLY POLY MAN

Hi,
Fatty! LAURA WALES
How do you
Hold up your pants?
Your   huge   Equator
Blancmanges   out   of   them
Jellymould   after   jellymould,
Your waistband   elastic
Cuts like wire in cheese:
Don't break in half —
You'll crush your
Own   two
Feet.

Dylan Thomas, and George Herbert with the added hazards of metre and rhyme, have proposed this agony to themselves in fine poems.

A more intricate torture is to play with letters instead of syllables:

I
am
any
dull
thing
within
eternal
pyramids
dispensing
cloistered

But you need to sedate yourself first.

George Herbert wrote a picture poem in the shape of angels' wings, and this idea was taken up again by Guillaume Appollinaire, who also wrote picture poems. Two of his most striking are, firstly, the little inverted heart in the shape of a candle-flame with the words 'My heart is a flame turned upside down'; and secondly, more susceptible to imitation, his poem about the rain in which the words trail down the page like raindrops.

You may also find snakes, lightning, rivers and scarves receptive to such treatment (as well as snow, hail, and universal darkness). The Muse, remember, is not responsible for our sanity.

I also include concrete poetry and sound poetry here. However elaborate the former may be, I think we should number it among our limbers, if not our doodles. Here is Edwin Morgan mixing us some concrete:

THE COMPUTER'S FIRST CHRISTMAS CARD

jollymerry
hollyberry
jollyberry
merryholly
happyjolly
jollyjelly
jellybelly
bellymerry
hollyheppy
jollyMolly
marryJerry
merryHarry

hoppyBarry
heppyJarry
boppyheppy
berryjorry
jorryjelly
moppyjelly
Mollymerry
Jerryjolly
bellyboppy
jorryhoppy
hollymoppy
Barrymerry
Jarryhappy
happyboppy
boppyjolly
jollymerry
merrymerry
merrymerry
merryChris
asmerryasa
Chrismerry
asMERRYCHR
YSANTHEMUM

Many concrete poets are not so easy to emulate. Stephen Morris, for example, seems to me to owe more to his experience as a graphic artist than to anything in literature. His work, fine though it is, is too elaborate to afford us any creative example as a writing game.

The Surreal Poem

This is a much more immediate proposition. We can either (in any form we choose, including free verse) open our mind to a series of images drawn from its bizarrest possibilities, pushing the imagination beyond 'lies' into nightmare, as the poet Mel Hardiment does here with a class in the East End of London:

IN THE LAND OF THE FLYING STEAMROLLERS

In the land where the flying steamrollers
Play leapfrog with bananas,
The sheep round up the sheepdogs
And gallop across their noses,

And steamrollers make love
With rusty screwdrivers.
Trees swim on their heads
And trains picnic in woods,
And cars race around in dustbins,
And pencils talk to each other,
The blackboards write sums
On tired teachers' faces.

Or we can choose a picture by Dali or Magritte, say, and write a fairly free description of what we see there:

An image of my grandmother
her head appearing upside-down upon a cloud
the cloud transfixed on the steeple
of a deserted railway station
far away

An image of an aqueduct
with a dead crow hanging from the first arch
a modern-style chair from the second
a fir-tree lodged in the third
and the whole scene sprinkled with snow . . .

This is not only liberating, and therefore useful as a limber, but it suggests a way of looking that may influence our other work. For example, here is a small poem that came straight out of such an exercise, while not being of the exercise:

HIGH CITY

In rooms stood on rooms overhead
there are grey men shaving
there are grey men shaving the clouds

and women with locks in their heads
afraid of moving
in case they walk into the sky

and teenage girls thinking boys
and both of them dreaming the sidewalk
where it's fast and away

from the ten million twenty million kids
shut up in boxes shut up in boxes
a tall pile of wall eyed boxes.

Simple rhyming forms

A warm-up should surely include working with these? We need one for amusement, and one to engage our mind.

The *limerick* is the obvious fun form:

> There was a young girl from Asturias
> Whose habits excited the curious:
> She used to throw eggs
> At her grand-mummy's legs
> Because their knock-knees made her furious.

It is a yeasty social challenge to make up a good bawdy limerick and slip it quietly into oral circulation and see how long it takes to crop up again.

Do you have the form? Here are a couple to complete if invention deserts you:

> There was an old sailor from Troon
> Who lay in his hammock till noon;
> At the end of his nap
> He dusted his cap
> And   (rhymes with Troon)

> A lady whose surname was Buckle
> Got bitten by bees on the knuckle
> And then on the nose
> (short line rhymes with nose)
> (long line rhymes with Buckle)

Our less abrasive form must be the ballad, I think. In all of its variations it provides the basis for perhaps a third of all the verse written in the English language, as well as for many folk- and pop-lyrics. It is, of course, the form I chose for the *Gunsmen* poem.

I am a rather bad rock-climber, so let us start climbing:

> Young Kev he climbed the mountainside
> As bold as bold could *be*,
> Till higher than the town he stood
> Taller than mast or *tree*.

Four stresses, three stresses, with only the three-stress lines needing to rhyme. Let us make the rhymes solid.

You may wish to start your own ballad-story (ballad is particularly suited to narrative, and to limber up with a ballad is a

47

good way of reminding us that our poetry ought to move), or you may care to follow me (and Young Kev) a little further:

> But still up rose the mountainside
> As mountainsides will do
> Through cliffs of cloud past cloudy cliffs,
> So Kevin rose up too

> Foot after foot, step after step
> And many a slip beside,
> Taller than forty steeples high,
> Giddy with dizzy pride . . .

Notice the simple narrative repetitions the ballad has made available to us these seven centuries, and reflect that when we deal in more sophisticated forms we may well need to put something in their place if our work is to have coherence.

Time for some more movement?

> Until he dazzled with the height,
> Grew frightened he would fall:
> 'Oh help me down, oh rescue me!'
> His brain began to bawl.

Notice the play on 'giddy', 'dizzy', and 'dazzled'; the ballad is spacious enough for us to develop this sort of verbal association. There is also a semantic connection of the sort that poetry delights in. The three words are all related, and the first two come from Sanskrit definitions of the nature of Godhead. Even in a joke poem, this fact may help its intellectual integrity.

> For all his wits were half-awry
> Through breathing breathless air.

(Primitive man found God in the high places, and he grew giddy/dizzy through seeking him; or he did if he lived near the Himalayas, where these words originate.)

Would you like to work out your own verse-rescue: another climber? a helicopter? a rock cave where he can rest? Or shall I indulge in one of those super-real (or surreal) devices that the play on *dizzy* and *deus* certainly allows us?

> Till the rock itself took hold of him
> And an eagle perched in his hair.

'Where am I, in what magic place
That the rockface guides my leg?'
Along of me, said the mountainside,
And the eagle laid an egg.

A ballad, in fact, provides a very relaxed arena in which we can
parade almost anything.

Lists, Palindromes and Backwords

Poets, as against novelists and biographers, have time to turn
words over and over and inside out. The simple acquisition of
words, book-browsing, specialist-manual-conning, dictionary- and
thesaurus-reading is very much a matter for poets. Novelists have
to do their research in such awful places as train-, bus-, and
aeroplane-timetables and the street-plans of cities.

Consequently, a poet's notebook fills itself with all kinds of lists
— words with similar derivations, rock-formations, words that
mean the same thing, swear-words, words we might one day use in
a poem if we ever decide to write like that, dead metaphors, fish
bones, words we could never use in a poem, and so on.

Some people, principally children and Herbert Read, have even
written list-poems. In Read's case the inspiration is refined to a
succession of single-word images (a list of words which are still live
metaphors, like 'throttle' as a noun or 'hammer' as a verb, would be
a good one for the notebook); and in the child's case the narrative
is reduced to a series of phrase-length pictures:

> boots in the grasses
> pop-eyed rabbit
> the sky opens
> blood on the footfall
> cartridges smoke

— a bit like that. The Anglo-Saxons did something quite similar, or
they did when they felt runic and gnomic; so I always think it is a
game worth playing.

As it happens, though, the kind of list I have most in mind for
such occasions is a list of palindromes, words that are the same
whether read forward or backwards. *Did dad pop a bib on Bab?*
And better still, those sinister words, 'backwords' I call them, that
make another word altogether when taken backwards, sly things
like *pal, stop, nip, Eros, emit,* and *snug.*

My notebooks are full of such nonsense. Then when I want to

rhyme without rhyming, and without placing myself in fee to
Wilfred Owen, in short when I want to play wordgames, I write a
backpoem, rhyming with backwords or backrhymes:

> Two happy fans, two neighbours, pals,
> Go strolling from the Match, the Game well won.
> The cold has numbed their fingers and their cheeks are raw:
> They demonstrate the shots that won the War
> Until one stumbles on the frost and now
> Falls flat-faced on the pavement with a slap.

A bit like Crabbe? Not too much like hard work, though; and it
must be exercising something.

Being Caliban

We do this with friends, of course. Some people are Caliban all the
time. Shakespeare had a go at Caliban's language. So did Browning.
So why shouldn't we? We simply write a Caliban poem (any form)
in invented vocabulary and syntax.

For a writing circle, or class, or cluster of writers recuperating
after a reading tour, there is an excellent variant of *Caliban*. I first
invented it for children, and called it *radio poem;* then I found that
adults could play it much more creatively, especially if the rules
were tightened. It is this. Take one of the great stories from
literature — *Gawain, Tristan,* even *Snow White and the Seven
Dwarves,* and apportion the episodes of the story, modified or not,
between you according to the numbers who want to take part.
Then each person writes a verse narrative (any form or
predetermined form) together with the necessary soliloquies or
speeches for his own episode. You then join the resulting narrative,
or recitative, or voice-drama together, and read it or perform it.
The leaven that can be added is to restrict the language-choice in
some way. Either there must be a limited vocabulary, or a heroic
vocabulary, or an invented or distorted vocabulary; or you can try
some version or other of a 'pure' vocabulary, for example a
vocabulary without adjective or adverb.

All of these constraints, or challenges, can be incorporated in
our solo exercises, of course; and they all help shape and strengthen
our approach to language and prosody.

At its most simple, *radio poem* can be written without constraint
as a group ballad. Even the most jaded brain should be able to
conjure one verse from the alcoholic haze.

There are those who say that nothing good will come of poets challenging one another, that the Muse 'does not like games.' Keats, Leigh Hunt and Shelley once played such a game, by proposing a sonnet on a set subject, the Nile. Leigh Hunt and Keats each produced admired sonnets, which were afterwards published. Shelley wrote *Ozymandias*. Naturally, he did as all poets do when they are midway through a writing exercise and find the Muse taking over: he let her. He allowed her to lead him from the rules a little, in this case the strict subject matter.

Spells

A fine poetic doodle (or piece of psychic irresponsibility according to our point of view) is to make a spell. A spell can take almost any physical form, but most spells are in verse because historically poetry was never far away from magic. A spell also allows us to experiment with language restraint (or be gigantically, grotesquely inventive), and, by its invocatory nature, throws us hard against the sound of words, and the selection of a vocabulary that is wise beyond its dictionary meaning. All spells, in fact, are written in some kind of Xanadu dialect or other.

Flyting

Dangerous to hurl spells at people, in case the stones listen and move; but a flyting is a fine desk sport. In it, we engage a fellow poet in a war of verse-insult; then invite him, by post or telephone, to reply in the same stanza form (rhyme is almost indispensable when we write lampoon or satire; and a neat verse adds zest to a laugh). Or we can have a fine communal flyting at the writing circle. Or we can sit in crabby solitude and write our adversary's answering scurrilities for him. This is a certain way of ensuring that we win.

Conceits

All poetry is prone to catch its death of conceit, so to toy with the following exercise is a way of placing ourselves on guard against the imagination's eagerness to overdo comparison. A conceit, as you know, is either a comparison that goes on too long or that starts by being too extravagant.

So, if we propose ourselves pigeons as a subject and stockbrokers as the point of comparison, the metaphor, then we might try something like this:

> Pigeons are city men who wear grey suits
> With nothing in their buttonholes and a cold-weather nose.
> They walk with hands folded at the back of their jackets
> And puffed-out chests with their heads on one side
> Or tucked into their collars, everything in place
> Save their toes poke through their boots and come in several colours.

Doing this makes us turn back to our subject, of course, and I find myself in error. Pigeons are straight-headed walkers in the main, so I slander them.

The next challenge is to tidy up the rhythm so it reads better; but that goes for all our exercises.

Conceits, like lies, make us re-examine the truth, so this is a useful writing exercise. They are simple to play with, yet keep our eye cocked in the right direction, towards meaning. Even if we toy with the other kind of conceit we are still on the boundaries of meaningful literature and may be driven to write some. At the least, we can examine two quite different sorts of rhetoric:

> Pigeons are city men who wear grey suits
> Or clog-footed firemen protected by asbestos.
> Toc-toc on the lawn I can see their clockwork strutting
> Like toddlers' model spacemen, like soldiers on parade,
> Till they stand close-footed as cabbages in frost
> Or bob together slowly like a bundle of balloons.

So much for writing games. Some of them are more than games, and others not the least bit funny. They all suggest their variables, and several will relate easily to all of the forms given at the end of the book. We never know when an exercise will turn into a poem, but we can be reasonably confident that from time to time it will. Inspiration is a matter of opening the mind. Everything else is work, and here we disguise work as play.

> *More* is more divine
> said the Immobile Horse.
> Furthermore, don't
> attempt to burden me
> with your encouragement.
> Ed Dorn *Gunslinger*

With reference to those lists of verse forms, they are all of them games, if you like, crosswords and jigsaws to solve with syllable and sound. Yet Gavin Ewart now says that he tries to find a fresh form for each new poem he writes, as a way of keeping invention fresh. At least he keeps his readers alert and watchful, and each poem quickens the wit. There are people who read poetry as if they are unravelling a cypher, and people who read it as if they are listening to God. Their pleasure, I suspect, is equal.

Chapter Six

'Does the road wind uphill all the way?'
'Yes, to the very end.'
'Will the day's journey take the whole long day?'
'From morn to night, my friend.'

Christina Rossetti

'I am going in seach of a great Perhaps.'

François Rabelais

1.

Our strategy is total. Our notebook is full, and — like Leonardo —
we are starting another. We have begun and will continue to
sharpen our written observation of matters that take our attention.
We have grown used to seeing some of those jottings as subjects
for a poem, and then as poems, so that we are ceaselessly
experimenting, shaping, pruning, rejecting, as we jot. At moments
that we shall continue to extend into minutes and then into hours,
the idea and the poem become synonymous, so that we now labour
to perfect, not to achieve. Our next target has become not the
ending, not even the perfected ending, but a better beginning.
Everything we do puts us in the way of this. We doodle in verse
rather than blots and blobs. We dream in words. We have an
arranged, or proclaimed, place of work. Sometimes, at least once
every day, we walk apart and are silent. We record what the
silence gives us, even if it is nothing.

We are not more intelligent than we were, more perceptive, nor
in a wider sense more knowledgeable. Poetry is not Pelmanism.
We know the small facts that glue themselves to our poems, that is
all. But the glue is good, and bonds tiny points of detail.

Nor are we better people — that least of all. We are probably
more ruthless, more selfish, more impatient. Or we hate ourselves

for not being so. We know what is before us, and we know there is not time enough for half of it.

We are more aware, and certainly more self-aware in the better sense of that expression. Our awareness extends to language, and we know that 'aware' is related to 'wary' and that 'wary' is a variant of 'on guard'. We have become wary and on guard with our social contacts. We still love and value them, but poetry was something we got by not talking, and that we cannot talk about. Like all writing, it can be talked away if we speak of it before doing it. Poetry is special, but it is not special in this.

Our self-awareness places us in an external world that has become in some senses unique. Our relationship with it has changed just sufficiently for us to feel a fresh valency in some if not all of its contents. We are their exponents, their advocates, their propagators even. That is our artistic ego, and it stands where it will not blind us. It relates to our personal world and not to the things we do in it, the best poems we can make.

We have begun to graft our ideas on to some kind of word-stock. The stock is increasingly ours, and all the better for planting.

We will plant it by concentrating on it, by determining what it is trying to grow to, by sensing its shape. Its perfect shape may elude us, so we are learning to solve this problem in a quite arbitrary manner that becomes less crude with practice.

Our strategy is for use, so it includes simplistic tactics. We may decide for example that every poem attempted will be in a certain form. So everything that we do will become an extended exercise, but an exercise aimed at sinking a rhythm into our blood until it gives back a poem.

I am sure the poem is there. The jottings, the false starts, the lies, the random jumble of metaphor, the writing games leading slowly to the fierce concentration on form that waits at the end of the book, the moments sitting apart, between them suggest its arrival.

It may already have written itself, springing up from what seemed a doodle and insisting you encourage it into the open. That is your hope and my faith. More likely you have had to work at it, painfully, hesitantly, piecemeal, clipping word to word, cross-referencing, erasing, until you could 'hear it'; and then the same bitter slog until you finished it.

Perhaps it is not yet finished.

You will finish it. Not out of faith or hope, but as an act of will. It will be worth it, worth it for the satisfaction that comes from making something; worth it for its own sake, and worth it the more if you can look it in the teeth, critically and fiercely, see its imperfections and resolve to set them aside in the next one. —

What a genius I had when I wrote that!

Jonathan Swift

I woke up and found myself famous.

Lord Byron

Chapter Seven

The very perfection of the house, as if Nature herself had made it, hides the builder's merit.

Thomas Carlyle *The Hero As Poet*

1.

The poem is made. Or it seems to be made. In other words we have solved all the problems we met in writing it.

Solved in our terms, that is. Our solutions may appal other people.

Then again, perhaps we solved the problems at the expense of the non-problems. We comfort ourselves by vanquishing the really troublesome difficulties — a couple of awkward rhymes, for example, an image that threatened to slip into the abyss — and overlook the needless repetition of a word, our acceptance of a cliché or *double-entendre,* all of which matters could be so easily remedied if only we could bring ourselves to notice them. Unnoticed, they detract totally from the poem and confuse its meaning.

Or we had a flawed poem, and we noticed the flaw and excised it, and the poem bled to death.

Then there is the problem beyond the poem, the problem that cannot be solved until a period of time has elapsed, the problem beyond the problems: why did we, why should anyone, write this poem?

Those earlier problems are practical ones, this philosophical, save it is difficult to envisage a practical solution to problems we do not even notice.

We need a confidant or confidante, a mentor. Ideally we need to find a poet who will read over our work and give advice. It needs to be the right poet, and a better poet than we are. If we become the best poets in the world, we still need to show our poems for comment and advice to someone we have learned to trust. Someone with a quick but constructive eye for our flaws, someone who is totally sympathetic to the way we go about things and appreciates what we are seeking to achieve. It is no good going to someone who wants to turn us into Shakespeare or, worse, into himself.

We must have such a person now. If we are tyros we must become sorcerer's apprentices. If we are journeymen poets we need to meet him occasionally for advice. If we are poets of accomplishment and find the idea of a tutor repugnant, then we should at least accept the chances that come our way to teach and encourage others. To instruct is to put ourselves forward, and in advancing beyond our normal social stance we may catch a glimpse of ourselves. In any event, we shall have to formulate our ideas and methods and examine their effect on others. Poetry, our sullen art, thirsts for dialogue.

2.

We also need one another.

It is helpful for a young poet to join a group or writers' circle. If there is not one in our area we should found one. If it becomes precious, we should leave it and found another. We should encourage factions, splinter-groups, cabals in the name of activity. Writers' circles attract the smug and the self-protective. They also encourage the dozy dogmatist; but it should only take one person of genuine will to bring the warring egos into a focus. All that is required ultimately is that people should listen to each other, grant a platform in return for a platform. It is good to temper our poetry in fierce, even wild or ribald criticism. To be read to a circle is often our poem's first publication. To hear it criticised will be depressing, stimulating, exasperating in turns — but at least we will see our work through others' eyes, and pick our way through valid and invalid comment.

If our talent is genuine and esoteric — and most of us think it is — then we may also learn that our poems repel or baffle people. They may not be understood, or understood but not admired, or understood and admired but not considered to be poetry.

This is important to know, the more so if we are serious in our longterm ambition and resolute in our aims. It is an awareness that should influence our creative strategy, especially when it comes to approaching publishers.

It also makes it even more imperative to find that sympathetic mentor, and find the right one moreover. Hopkins of all people had such a need, but he only found Robert Bridges.

58

3.

The next activity our writing circle should be chivvied towards is the anthologising of its members' work. Once a year, or once a quarter, it should produce and sell one of the variants between printed book and bound stencil or photocopy that its wealth, which is our wealth, can support. If we are not selected for inclusion we demand democracy. Once we become editors we insist on standards and let the mediocre go to the wall. This anthology is our first real step towards the daylight, and moves a small way towards little magazines and the local art presses. The more writing circles we belong to at any one time, the more steps we can take, of course, but the more expensive they are likely to be.

When we have written a number of poems we shall probably want to see them published. Indeed, publication may well extend our further development. If we write public poetry, it needs to be made public. If we think we are merely solitary scribblers, perhaps that assumption needs to be tested as well. Offering our work up in this way adds an entirely new dimension to our powers of self-criticism. It releases some pressures just as surely as it increases others. Is it publication that frightens us, or being refused publication? Poetry is not the most marketable of commodities, so there will be plenty of refusals.

Each time we receive a rejection slip we shall be in good company.

> I could not use them to paper the walls. No building, *no* building, was strong enough to withstand the weight.
> E. Corbett *Down the Ladder of Literary Success*

We can find out the national periodicals that publish poetry by walking into the reading room of our local library. The little magazines are myriad, and they come and go. They can be found by paying a visit to a specialist bookshop (they also come and go, but there is one under an archway somewhere in most major cities).

59

4.

Then comes the matter of the first selection of verse: publication in book form. For some reason it is always spoken of as a first collection, but it is bound to be a selection in fact, for all of the reasons of drafting, finalising, and general uncertainty that we have considered.

When I was young, I was warned by an aunt of mine who knew about such matters, 'not to rush into print'. She was right. She would not be right now, so if at any point in your career you sense the floodgates about to open, make no attempt to hold back your coracle. Chances do not come often; or, to put the point more positively, you are as likely to have a second chance if you muff your first one as if you refuse it.

If you have time — and I am afraid that poets tend to have more time than they need: constantly baulked at the weir, with the lock gates incessantly closed to them — if you or I have time, it is good to seek some kind of harmony of theme in a first book. Ideally, of course, we should be looking for this throughout our writing, but nothing is quite ideal. Your strategy, though, should be to make your voice accumulate in the publisher's mind. What you offer must seem intelligent, planned and professional, not a random collection of occasional pieces. If you have worked hard at yourself these years and are confident that your voice and viewpoint will be the harmonising element, then you can afford a looser collection, but you will be making large claims for yourself. Still, we all have to put our best forward and we can as easily lance the giant as tilt at a windmill.

In talking about the publication of poetry, I wish to discuss the world as it really is today, not as the manuals for writers pretend it is. Some of the things I shall say will in consequence be totally shocking to professional writers, to the half of me that writes novels, and to my agent. My agent will at least know that I offer no falsehoods.

Entirely different standards operate in the publication of poetry than in the publication of everything else. So whatever you do as a poet seeking publication do not attempt to stand on your rights. You have none. You had rights sitting at your desk before you decided to publish. Now you have none. You have the fool's right, merely, the right to say 'no'. But you are here to say 'yes'. That being said, a reputable publisher is not going to try to swindle you. The publication of poetry is positively the one transaction over which a reputable publisher will *not* attempt to swindle you. Why should he snatch back the pennies he has just dropped in the beggar's hat? So hold your tongue and know your place and you may grow up to be one of those few poets who can dictate terms and quibble over contracts, because they can actually sell books. There are two such poets in England, and perhaps as many again in the States.

This is not to say that you cannot make money writing poetry; you can. With a little organisation you can even make enough to live off, through readings and appearances and so on. Before you rush headlong in that direction, though, it is worth reflecting that the people who are totally successful make performance a full-time career, spend their days commuting between London, Scotland and the West Coast of America, and very rarely get to see their families or books or, ever again, the Muse.

So if an accredited publisher accepts your book on the basis of your guaranteeing the sale of a certain number of copies, or a *quid pro quo,* your providing a book on another subject (this sort of proposition is most likely to come to an academic or journalist rather than an ordinary mortal) say 'yes', provided you have enough money to underpin your confidence, or enough interest in the proposed subject. Forget the old-fashioned advice about authors never paying to be published. You are not an author anyway, but a poet, something both higher and lower, but in any case different. You are not marketing *The Sex Life of Adolf Hitler* or *The Dog Lover's ABC*. Even if you lack the money and the interest, you should still say 'yes'. You serve not honour but the Muse.

I should like to stress again that I am talking about offers made by national commercial publishing houses, not — for the moment — vanity publishers. It is unusual for commercial houses to make such an offer, but I know of three who do or have done; and, as the Idiot observed, 'Times are changing all the time.' I foresee no time when 'times' will be better for publishers or poets.

Certainly a contingent offer from such a publisher is not to be scorned. Whatever deal he strikes, books will only appear on his list because he believes in them.

The usual counter-cry — you will hear it when you return in triumph to your writing circle, or wherever your bays are paraded — is that 'a book should be good enough to stand on its own two feet.' In fact, most of the major poets in the English language have, since the dawn of time, been signally bad at producing books that stand on their own two feet, at least initially. They nearly all owed publication, especially their early publication, to wealth, patronage or subscription. Subscription is commonly held to mean no more than selling in advance of production; but in fact we all know that it is in reality selling by blackmail. We sign a subscription list to help poor So-and-So get off the ground. We don't want his beastly book. We want him to take his whining little smile somewhere else. Subscription selling is not even blackmail. It is begging. That being said, I am absolutely in favour of poets being beggars, providing we and the world are clear about it.

In the United Kingdom a number of poets have books assisted by the Arts Council, by its regional branches or by private charities; so I fail to see any difference. The poet has been subsidised while he has been writing his book, and then the publisher has been subsidised to help the costs of production. If a poet involves himself in such a scheme, or as much of it as he can get (and he would be a fool not to) then the result is subsidised publishing. It is crass to pretend otherwise, and not to pretend otherwise provides us with very good ammunition back at the writing circle.

Similar situations apply at some university presses in the United States. Poetry is not produced on a commercial basis but because the press wishes to be associated with this kind of venture. I have heard American academic poets boast 'they need us because we lend them tone.' They do not say it when their publishers are at hand. Tone has never been a currency in any kind of bargain, except when aristocracy is forced to marry wealth.

I am only being churlish at everyone's expense because I wish to stress this single point. As poets we cannot bargain, only bluff.

In Western Europe and the United States, and perhaps in other countries too where a caring for the literary arts is a largely subterranean activity, there is a two-tier system at work. Firstly there are the major publishing houses, the general list publishers who still like to leave a poet for politeness on the edge of their plate. Then there are the specialised poetry presses — 'little presses' is an insulting misnomer when we consider how long and distinguished some of their lists are.

We must make ourselves known to these and to the editors of the university and subsidised presses before we accept that our books will not be published. By the time this happens, it will be time to begin at the start of the chain again, with fresh work or at least a new title and a different arrangement (and, of course, a clean typescript). Editors move too, of course, though their employment prospects are nearly as low as ours. So we may find a chink in the armour. We may be lucky enough to have our poems read before being returned this time. We may half stick in a half mind as someone who may be worth half watching for the future.

Then there is 'vanity publishing', that is, the offer of a press (it is unlikely to be either national or 'little') to publish your book if you foot the bill. This is quite different from a partnership deal, or a guarantee, or a *quid pro quo*. The publisher making the offer, or more likely advertising his availability to fulfil your commission in this way, is pretty certainly making his whole living in this manner. So the 'bill' will include a proportion of his overheads and profit, as well as his winter holiday.

So why not consider becoming your own publisher? You will save some of your money, and you will certainly be expressing your commitment to your poetry. You must find your own printer, enlist the aid of a designer (from the local art or technical college?), get a costing and then, if feasible, go ahead. You will then have a book to give to friends and to sell to audiences whenever you appear at a poetry reading.

The poetry reading, the public poetry reading that is, is a form of publication, of course. The art of publication by declamation has a noble lineage running through the border balladeers, Chaucer and the troubadours of Languedoc right the way back to Homer. Over the last twenty years it has flourished again to offer the one really lively marketplace for poetry in the Western World. It is a forum which not only pays poets to read or recite their poems, but actually offers them a chance to be their own booksellers and peddle their wares direct to the audience. A number of major publishing houses are happy enough for this to happen, and so are most of the little presses. If you are your own publisher, of course, you can sell without restraint. In theory the major publishers are infringing a trade agreement with their booksellers, but the proliferation of paperjacket outlets has caused this to become blurred of late. Anyway I know of no bookseller to whom any poet owes anything, except the penury-ridden specialist booksellers whose trade can only be enhanced by a good poetry-reading in the area.

Just a last note, in fairness. There are some vanity publishers who are worth considering, though you would need to explore their credentials with extreme caution. If there is money enough, but too little time, health or energy, then doubtless they have a role to play. They may release a pressure that is otherwise intolerable.

> So we, that earst were wont in sweet accord
> All places with our pleasant notes to fill,
> Whilest fauorable time did vs afford
> Free libertie to chaunt our charmes at will:
> All comfortlesse vpon the bared bow,
> Like wofull Culuers doo sit wayling now.
> > Edmund Spenser *Euterpe* from
> > *The Teares of the Muses*

The certainty would have to be that they are genuinely selective about what they publish (as distinct from pretending to be selective); do present the author with a properly produced book; and do have distribution outlets. These are likely to be more limited than a commercial publisher's, and less geared to poetry than a specialist publisher's.

The most important question of all is: how energetically will they advertise and send out copies for review? Poetry needs to be published, not locked up in print and forgotten.

Chapter Eight

Frivolity is out of season.
Yet, in this poetry, let it be admitted
The world still needs piano-tuners
And has fewer, and more of these
Gray fellows prone to liquor
On an unlikely Tuesday . . .
          Margaret Avison *The World Still Needs*

1.

Poetry is for causal not casual users of words. Yet we can grow tired of being so deliberate. Practise, certainly, but we dull ourselves by too much practice, whether at poetry directly, or by filling our notebooks, inventing complicated verse-exercises or dreaming of stimulants. What we need to do is study. Study the world we want to write about, study other poets. The poet is not only a hunter but a cannibal. He does not crib, nothing as innocent as that. How can he crib? To take another's work on trust would be to accept his version of the world. But if he does not crib, he does not ignore other men's and women's poetry either. He seizes it and chews it to the bone, and like a person who has eaten a good meal he is modified by what he eats. The world's libraries are full of miraculous poems, and we need to be filled with their cadences if the transcendent rhythm is to compose itself in our dreams. We need to read our contemporaries, including foreign poets in translation, to be aware of the possibilities of the age. When we have sifted them all, and weighed and weighted them against our own version of the world, we may be aware of a viewpoint they have missed, subjects they have overlooked. And there, suddenly, there will be something waiting for us to give it expression, a whole poem sitting on a shoulder and getting ready to sing to us.

To be constantly employing our craft — I say it again — is to dull it. There is so much we can do, no more. After that, we have to wait for poetry to happen.

Inspiration is not confined to poets in particular, nor to wordsmiths at large. But a poet's inspiration has to be a broader and more intense stroke of lightning: it has to illuminate the forest, not set fire to a single tree. It is an inspiration which at its finest has to show up and purify the whole of language, setting words in their order and degree. To read a great poem is not only to be awestruck at what is there, the way the impossibilities are matched, but to be equally devastated by what is left out, the mere possibilities that have been summoned up in their droves to lurk beyond the edges of the text, all the echoes, all the allusions, all the curt dismissals. So to read the complete work of a major poet is like seeing the entire landscape of words during a violent electric storm.

Words can be freshest if we take a genuine interest in them for their own sake. If we look after words, they will look after us when the time comes. We have already noted the poet's witplay in our ballad exercise, the careful appositions (and appositeness) of ear and eye relationships in the verses by Hopkins and Auden, the arrogant use the poet makes of language in general. Yet is arrogance at work, or is it something more akin to a familiarising reverence? The arrogance is towards the subject, not to the words; or towards the reader, who must be jarred constantly to watchfulness. No, the poet is courteous with words, and in order to pay them the proper respect he needs to know something of their background and pedigree.

Some poets have been lucky enough to study the semantics of a major European language before coming to poetry, or to have done research among early archive material, or to have read Classics. The rest of us are going to need a fairly close acquaintance with one of the detailed histories of the English language, the sort that deals with words rather than generalities, if we are to get on terms with the job. We shall need a good etymological dictionary at our elbow, too; but then we always need that.

You may think that all of this fiddle is not for you. I think you will be wrong. It is possible that you know enough already, of course. Or that you do not understand what I am talking about. Here are three simple questions I often pose to writing classes, and always to language groups:

1. Can you relate the names of the days of the week to the relevant Germanic Gods, and through them to their parallel Graeco-Roman Gods and their associated planets?

2. Can you derive the names of the months of the year?

3. Do you know anything (other than family hearsay, an important commodity in other contexts) about the derivation of your own name and the other family surnames, and the more salient local place names?

These questions are arbitrary enough, but they point towards a dimension, and they indicate it by means of some of the most common words in our language. To find the answer to these will involve us in other questions and a deepening awareness of language's resonance. It is impossible, for example, for me to say *Tuesday* and not see the God's bitten hand, the Fenris Wolf and the miraculous chain that ensnared him, followed by images of Ragnarok, the dreadful day of his escape, and then associate them with Mars, Tuesday's Planet and Tir's double in the Roman pantheon. There is an entire story in even the Germanic elements of that one word, as well as an allegory for the endless cycle of order and chaos. There was once a poem for me too, and as I type this I can glimpse another one. This may seem like tedious work, but how else can we find words that glitter?

Am I saying that we should behave like a seventeenth or eighteenth century reader of Milton and familiarise ourselves with every classical reference? Not a bit of it (though we could do much worse). I merely suggest that we should add this interest in their pedigree to our overall awareness of words.

Tomorrow is always hidden under a stone marked *Yesterday* and yesterday has many stones. This sudden discovery of something new in the old is as true of historical linguistics as it is of the semantics of form. There may be nothing new under the sun: nor is there anything so old that it can be assumed to be in total decay. If we turn from books to the language of our chosen world, whether it be psychiatry, freshwater fishing or automobile engineering, we are in the presence of rich *arcane* vocabularies. The average workshop manual for a motor car, for example, will contain some four thousand words we do not normally meet in everyday life: twice the vocabulary of the French classical tragedians.

These words are immaculate, too, untouched by literature and largely unqualified by allusion. They are nouns, just as all names are nouns. Poetry needs nouns, not tricksy words like adjectives and adverbs. To lie intimately under a car, and drop down its gearbox is to find oneself among an elect order of cones, roller-races, needle-rollers, lay-shafts and shims. We need more nouns in the language, because it is nouns that make metaphor, nouns that are metaphor. I will willingly trade 'shim' for any adjective under the sun, even an interesting adjective like 'buxom' that has reversed

67

its meaning in two centuries, but become very tired in the process, or 'wan' that has turned turtle in ten.

It is normally said that 'a little learning is a dangerous thing.' A little learning can greatly enrich our attitude to language, and is a whole lot better than none.

What, though no mice are caught by a young kitten,
May it not leap and play as grown cats do,
Till its claws come?

Shelley *The Witch of Atlas*

2.

This avoidance of overkilling our poetry is not an evasion of work, then. We substitute research for practice, that is all. There is always plenty to do in the knowledge that one is a poet, even though no poems have come for a very long time. Poetry is either work or patience, generally both. That has been my theme so heavily and so persistently that it has become as dull as any similar injunction. And because it is morally attractive to speak sourly of work we are in danger of overlooking the value of patience. Poetry like fishing is a waiting game. If you cannot wait, take up fishing — coarse-fishing preferably, because it resembles poetry in its dour waiting for the unlikely to happen — or some other activity that develops a relaxed attitude to time.

More than that, take up some other form of writing. I do not agree with Eliot that Hardy and Lawrence would have been better poets if they had not written novels. Given all of the circumstances of their lives they were probably better poets for having written novels. If you take up another form of writing, so that your desk can continue its habits with you, then you are likely to find your poetry will feed off your novels or biographies, not the other way about.

Make up your mind whether you want to be a lover or a writer of love poetry.

A father's letter to his son

If you manage to produce another book that is saleable, its existence will change every publisher's view of you as a poet. They will no longer think of you as a poet. They will think of you as that promising author who unfortunately writes poetry. They will ask to see your poetry and turn it down with the utmost friendly reluctance while encouraging you to write an even more saleable book to follow your first saleable book. You bargain with this second book. You are now in a position to ask for your own *quid pro quo*. You sneak behind your agent's back and deliberately allow your publisher to erode your advance on the second book, so that the poetry may be subsidised, not from charity but from your own pocket. You will happily take two thousand pounds instead of seven, just so you can see your love affair with the Muse decently acknowledged in print. You then go to your agent and get him to claw the five thousand back again, but only when the poems have been set up in type. You will still not be seen as a poet, but as a smart operator whose poetry we publish. You will no longer have to say 'yes' to people. You will have a strategy. You may even find that you are not a poet at all.

I intend to be a lover as well as a writer of love poetry. That being said, I think I shall find scant time to become a romantic novelist as Aunt Edna suggests. Can you find me a partnership somewhere in the business, preferably half-time?

A son's letter to his father

Chapter Nine

True ease in writing comes from Art, not Chance,
As those move easiest who have learned to dance.
'Tis not enough no harshness gives offence,
The sound must seem an echo to the sense.

Alexander Pope An Essay on Criticism

1.

The poem's language weighs upon the poet from a number of directions. There is its metre, if any, and in any event its rhythm; its stanza, if any, with the pressure of rhyme; its rhetoric, its syntax, and its imagery and symbol. They constantly demand his attention and practice. They are all rubbed equally into the dough, but at least rhetoric and syntax do not need call for too much general thought, however galling they can be.

Syntax is a grammatical description of the way words are arranged in sentences. As poets we write in sentences, even though they may be sentences in rhyme and metre. The best, probably the only, precept we can follow is always to write sentences in our poems that meet the requirements of good contemporary prose. It is the surest way to free our work of archaisms, pretence and fake artifice. Look at the four lines by Pope at the top of this chapter. They have an unforced natural order. If we cannot match their deceptive simplicity, or be entirely 'prose-like', we ought to make sure that our departure from the norm seems natural to the context, so it sounds like 'a newer prose' rather than old verse.

Rhetoric is the ordering of words for maximum effect. It might be called applied syntax, and in fact it is generally extended to embrace every figure of speech except for that part of imaginative language we rather vaguely call imagery. Imagery itself is language used 'for effect', so in a sense it is also a part of rhetoric. It is tempting to say that rhetoric is only to do with structures, the way words, and indeed sentences, are assembled, 'applied syntax' as I suggested; but there are figures of speech — 'metonymy' and 'synecdoche', for example — which sometimes relate to single words. Still, it is a rough guide to understanding a pantechnicon expression.

Of course a poet will develop his own 'rhetoric', his own way of assembling language for effect. The way his words, and with them ideas, tend to arrange themselves is what we mean by his style.

I do not think we need to waste time with accounts of the different forms of rhetoric. Each time we wrestle with a poem, we try to make rhetoric work for us. Every time we read somebody else's poem we look to see how it is done. To stumble across a new stanzaic pattern or syllabic possibility is enough for some poets to find a poem. I do not see any poems, or any enhanced writing, coming from a long list of figures of speech and rhetorical devices, though. Either they are live, in which case we use them in our everyday language and know them, even if not their names, or they are dead.

The linguistic necrophiliac will be able to find them all, with examples, in any old-fashioned grammar book.

Why is this thus? What is the reason of this thusness?
Artemus Ward His Book

2.

The image is a different matter. It strikes to the raw heart of poetry. Fortunately we have already been working with it. We spoke of the ear and eye relationships in a passage from Hopkins and another from Auden. In our verse exercises we played with conceits, a too-lengthy comparison between pigeons and city men; a series of over-elaborated comparisons between pigeons and balloons and cabbages. The first sort of conceit was an extended metaphor. The second was a hotch-potch of metaphors and similes. They are 'pictures', sometimes sensual, and if so not merely connected with seeing, sometimes intellectual, which a cluster of words transfer to the brain. An image may also be a conceit — we have seen how — or a symbol. A symbol is a returning point of reference, such as Yeats' obsession with the gyre, the conic flight from the wrist and then back to the lure of the trained bird of prey. This is both a metaphor, because Yeats implies a comparison between it and other concerns, the world's disorder for example, and a symbol, because he returns to it on a number of occasions and uses it as a kind of shorthand for all of the richness of meaning it has come to bear.

When I was sixteen I went around hunting for symbols. Every great poet had to have his symbols, I felt, so that great critics could write books about his symbolism. It was only when I left off reading what Roy Campbell called 'books about books about books' that my quest slackened. A good thing too. We must avoid making our poetry turgid with abbreviated meaning, and nothing is more calculated to slow it down than the presence of words that clearly mean (but fail to mean clearly) more than they say.

> His gob like a portcullis clenched
> As if to shut out care . . .
>
> Anon

A symbol plants itself, if it ever does, somewhere among a bulk of writing. Some poets begin to find that their imaginative landscape has recognisable points of return. When this happens they can collate their symbols. To have no symbols to collate does not mean we have failed. If we keep on casting about for them we shall never get any work done.

People who write books about books are much better at finding that sort of thing than people who merely write books. Besides, our task is each single poem.

3.

A simile makes a comparison by using the words 'like' or 'as'. It says, rather than implies, that two concepts are similar. Easy examples are Flecker's ships that 'sail like swans asleep' or Barker's 'hand like five bananas on the shoulder' (you may think that the latter is also a conceit); and Poe's, 'thy beauty is to me/ As those Nicean barks of yore.'

Metaphor does not compare. Or rather it does not signal, by using 'like' or 'as' that it is about to effect its own condensed form of comparison. It simply goes ahead and describes something in terms of something else. It may, for example, talk about the sun as if it were a flower:

The sunset's petals drowned across the bay

or:

The last petals of daylight drowned in the water

or, more abbreviated:

The petals drowned. It was dark.

I have chosen high-flown examples because they teach us to be on our guard. Metaphor constantly crowds upon metaphor (as it does in speech), and unless we are careful the metaphors will not come from the same area of the imagination. The ear-and-eye link will become broken somewhere along the chain, and the poem sag.

For example, each of the above lines contains a second metaphor: *drowned*. Strictly, petals do not drown. Yet 'drown' is a common word, unobtrusively applied. We have become perfectly happy for anything that gets wet to drown: logs, crops, eyes, embers or hillsides. It is halfway, in short, to becoming a dead metaphor. As poets we do not like dead metaphors. We object to cliché. But if we try to substitute a live metaphor the chance is that the entire description will become too rich, too discordant.

This throws up a general rule about revision. The purpose of cutting is to prune an idea back to its essentials. This is fine in prose, but in poetry we are left with a break in the rhythm, a hole in the stanza. We tend, if we cut one image, to look around for another that will bear the same weight. In fact, though, this new image will be padding. We need to introduce an entirely new idea. The stanza with its words slimmed should be able to hold more, not be made up of an uneasy mixture of wit and cottonwool.

It was J. Middleton Murry who said that metaphor is both more poetic and dramatic than simile, because it is more condensed. An inference seems to have been drawn from this remark that a good writer should change all of his similes into metaphors, tighten his metaphors into adjectives and then get rid of his adjectives entirely. It is a good recipe for pure writing, but not much else.

If Murry was contrasting the slowfootedness of words with the quick flight of the imagination, then he had a point. If he was suspicious of decoration and saw metaphor as the figure that was fast enough to keep up with its subject matter, then he had another. But in truth it is silly to malign poor old simile. It is, after all, the natural way to compare like with like. It gives the brain time to act on the new information and settle it into its onward appreciation of the poem. Often, too, the modern poet is comparing like with unlike — Barker's 'hand like five bananas' is an example of this — and the outrageous takes time to sink in.

I know of no better instance of the natural, contrasting uses of metaphor and simile than those Ted Hughes gives us in an early poem of his called *Wind:*

The tent of the hills drummed and strained its guyrope

an easy developed metaphor, followed equally easily by the simile:

The house
Rang like some fine green goblet in the note
That any second would shatter it.

First follow Nature, and your judgement frame
By her just standard, which is still the same:
Unerring Nature, still divinely bright,
One clear, unchanged and universal light,
Life, force, and beauty must to all impart,
At once the source, and end, and test of Art.
Alexander Pope *An Essay on Criticism*

Pope meant something different by 'Nature', but he will do us very nicely on imagery.

4.

In the arguments developed from Murry's proposition, we encounter a dislike of all embellishment, the adjective most of all.

The fewer adjectives we use the better. Adjectives are generally dead metaphors anyway, and very slippery of meaning. They also tend to offer themselves to us as easy padding to plump out metre and stanza. It is, if you like, very hard to say anything surprising with an adjective. The obvious adjectives are always tautologous and the less obvious ones stand out as so many plushy additives. Why, as the old poet said, write about a rose if all you can say about it is that it is red?

If we think of the thunderous openings of John Donne's poems, we find that adjectival movements play no part in them:

> Mark but this flea, and mark in this
> How little that which thou deniest me is:
> It suck'd thee first and then suck'd mee . . .

or:

> For Godsake hold your tongue and let me love . . .

Once Donne has established a stanza, he can use an adjective very tellingly because of the selective weight his frugality gives it. (He writes the whole opening stanza, seventy syllables, of *The Good Morrow*, without using a *descriptive* adjective at all.) I think of *Aire and Angels*:

> Twice or thrice had I loved thee
> Before I knew thy face or name;
> So in a voice, so in a *shapeless* flame,
> Angells affect us oft, and worship'd be . . .

Then again, in *Song,* after eight lines of impossible commands we are asked:

> What winde
> Serves to advance an *honest* mind

and we realise that this most formidable list has been constructed solely to promote the merits of that simple adjective. Donne does not despise adjectives, then. He hoards them and spends them as the rare gold they are. This is how we should use them. As I said, the fewer we use the better.

Auden at first sight is an over-user of adjectives; but in fact he too treasures their possibilities, and advances them outrageously:

> Underneath the abject willow

or more arrogantly still:

> The shining neutral summer has no voice
> To judge America or ask why a man dies.

His adjectives are as active as verbs. They are not merely

descriptive, or static: they increase what we know about the poem's centre:

> Lay your sleeping head, my love,
> Human or my faithless arm . . .

Then again, he uses adjectives like 'fashionable' and 'boring' in the same poem, because by his own methods he makes us respect their weight, just as much as Donne does by his frugality.

There are two modest, practical exceptions I can offer to the general advice of staying away from adjectives until we are confident in our art. A long time ago I wrote a one-dimensional poem of obvious movement and limited resource called *Hunting With A Stick*. In its opening lines it too stays away from adjectives, until it feels it has earned the right to use them. But it does use a present participle as an adjective (always a much more *active* sounding usage), and it uses a noun (more *concrete*, dare I say?):

> Once ten years old in the cobweb sun
> I chased a rabbit on stiffening grass
> Till it twinkled into its hole of sand.
> Although I knew that the hunt was done
> (For rabbits burrow deeper than fire)
> I crouched and crept there, stretching my hand;
> And kneeling my shadow on frost I saw
> In a turn of the hole too tight to pass . . .

Apart from my participle adjective and my noun as adjective the poem runs for eight lines until 'tight', and tight is not a descriptive adjective, but in its own small way just like many of Donne's: absolutely necessary to meaning.

It lives by violence and dies by liberty . . .
Always it desires to spend itself

Leonardo da Vinci *Force*
from *The Notebooks*

We discussed the difficulties that attend rhyming in an earlier chapter. Those same problems are there if we use some of rhyme's favoured substitutes, whether we call them half-rhymes, para-rhymes or backwords.

There are many ways in which words can relate without fully rhyming.

They can *nearly* rhyme, e.g. *bash* and *catch* or, even more closely, the famous *islands* and *silence* — we have to be very precise in speech to make that pair sound different.

They can have a vowel relationship: *hay, mate, sail,* etc.

Or they can have a consonant relationship: *moon, dun, spin.* The consonant relationship can be strengthened by making all of the consonants in monosyllables match: *moon, moan, mean, main* or *sport, spurt.* If we move to bisyllabics, then there are relationships like *curtain, cotton, kitten.*

A long, stressed syllable *trees* can relate to a short, stressed syllable *tress*; or we can make an unstressed syllable mist*ress* relate to a stressed syllable *dress.* The philosophers of this method claim that if the stress follows the unstress then the result is an optimistic, 'upward' sound. If it is the other way about, they say it is a depressing, 'downward' sound. They speak of 'rising' or 'falling' rhymes.

Then we can write hard rhymes, or any of the above, in which we break one or both of the rhyming words between two lines, making the natural enjambment split the words in half — *carve* with *harv*est.

If we want to write contemporary rhyming verse, the chance is that all of the above, and my 'backwords', will either force themselves upon us or be affected by us as mannerisms. It is worth remembering two things. The first is that using less than hard rhymes will not absolve us from meeting the requirements of intelligence and taste we discussed in an earlier chapter. The second is our awareness of a small historical quibble. All of our experimenting with rhyme arose because down the years poets have allowed themselves to rhyme by precedence. Such rhymes as *war/jar, mind/wind* (the blustery noun not the twisting verb) came to be called 'eye rhymes', even though some of them (e.g. Shakespeare's 'daughter' and 'after' in *Lear*) do not work for the eye any more than they now work for the ear. The fact is they worked once, before changes of pronunciation forced them apart. Perhaps, then, it is worth rhyming properly or not at all.

Double rhymes e.g. *laughter/after* in modern English are normally, not exclusively, the property of light verse. Polysyllabics e.g. *Ermyntrude/sperm intrude* almost always are.

With polysyllabics, half-rhymes can strike up a stronger relationship. *Elephant* gongs well with *irrelevant* (in pop songs it even mates with *telephone*). The making of multiple rhymes between a polysyllable and several words, or more words than one, is a further humorous device, especially in the bawdy limerick. The Bishop of *Buckingham* (of blessed memory) could only be thought of as doing one thing to *'em,* though *chucking 'em/sucking 'em/* and *ducking 'em* also lurch into view.

There is an exception to every rule, generally furnished by a genius. Browning makes the most hideously serious point when he stresses *promise* (the whole ethos of *The Pied Piper*) by rhyming it with *from mice,* the rodent plot of the poem. But then Browning can rise in triumph above most conventions.

Poetry should surprise by a fine excess and not by Singularity.

Keats *Letter to J. H. Reynolds*

Chapter Ten

> I wish our clever young poets would remember my homely
> definitions of prose and poetry; that is, prose = words in their
> best order; poetry = the best words in the best order
>
> Coleridge *Table Talk*

1.

Metre, rhyme and stanza are not words that we can ignore, however
fashionable it may be to do so. Our individual poems may be
within or without them; but they are lines drawn on the map of
verse, if not of poetry itself, and they cannot simply be overlooked.

There is a pulse to be sought in free verse, of course; and I talk
about it later. It has always seemed to me the easier to find
because I was grounded in this other, more intransigent landscape
by people who taught me rules. I had to learn for myself that there
are no rules, but some very daunting descriptions.

Metre is the word used to describe the way verse works in its
smallest real unit, the line. To *describe,* not to insist that this is the
only way it can work.

To do this, it first tries to measure the length of the line, by
counting its stresses, or its long syllables, or simply its syllables;
then it describes the rhythmic units it pretends that the line is
composed of. It calls these units feet.

English feet concern themselves with stressed and unstressed
syllables, normally notated / and ✕.

The snag is that some continental measures, including a number
of forms that have found their way into English, are concerned
with long and short syllables, generally notated ‒ and ◡.

Many of the clearest, that is the falsest, rules of prosody are to
be found in school grammar books. Historically, these books were
written by scholars well-grounded in Latin; and they often scan
English verse with long and short signs as if it were Latin. Hence a
certain amount of unnecessary confusion. It is useless to turn to
more modern text books for clarification, because two newer, and

correcter, grammatical theories have enveloped English studies, with the odd result that school grammarians now find it safer to teach nothing. Poets under the age of forty can go back to the beginning with a mind totally uncluttered by many forms of useful knowledge.

Here are the English feet, correctly notated, but with their usual Graeco-Roman names:

The *iamb*   (or iambic foot): a light, unaccented, or unstressed syllable, followed by a heavy, accented or stressed syllable: x / e.g. 'attémpt'.

(I am now going to talk only of stressed and unstressed, this being what the other mouthfuls mean.)

The *trochee* (or trochaic foot): a stressed followed by an unstressed syllable: / x e.g. 'mattĕr'.

The *anapaest* (or anapaestic foot): x x / there are very few anapaestic *words* in English, which tends to front- stress its polysyllables; so here is a line by Browning, commonly stressed as anapaestic.

I spráng|tŏ thĕ stírr|ŭp, ănd Jór|ĭs, ănd hé;

You will notice, though, that the first foot is an iamb. Indeed, the whole poem only has one line that begins with an anapaest and maintains anapaests throughout, and there are other half-stresses and confused syllabic weights which run counter to the anapaest's so-called galloping rhythm.

The *dactyl*   (or dactylic, or dactylaic foot): a stressed followed by two unstressed syllables: / x x e.g. 'édĭblĕ'.

Note: there are many dactylic words in English, probably the majority of our unprefixed three-syllabled words, in fact. These are less clear-cut if one is an American (see later). But in scanning, the break between feet does not have to come at a word end. There is often a very real tension between the way the line *should* scan in order to fit the metre and the way it would scan if read as ordinary speech. A good metricist can exploit the pull between these two forces. A bad one allows metre and speech-stress to drift so far apart that the verse collapses.

There are two more feet, one of them rare as the substance of a whole poem, the other real enough but incapable of forming the basis of an entire line, let alone a poem. The rare one first:

The *amphibrach:* unstressed followed by a stressed followed by an unstressed syllable, e.g. x / x e.g. 'intrepid'. Bridges and Flecker both claim to have written amphibrachs. I cannot scan their poems this way. The amphibrach seems to lose itself among dactyls and anapaests, confused enough territory already.

The *spondee*   (or spondaic foot): two stressed (in origin, two long syllables together): / / e.g. 'hubub'. Many poems have 'a spondaic' movement in part of the line, e.g. 'Troy's doomladen shore', but it is impossible to sustain for long, and it often blurs into the more formal needs of the metre of the whole poem. It is a metric device, rather than a metre.

> You shall see them on a beautiful quarto page where a rivulet of text shall meander through a meadow of margin.
> Sheridan *School for Scandal*

As I mentioned earlier, these feet group together in regular units to make lines. Almost certainly a given line will contain irregularities — inversions and elisions or 'a spondaic movement'. A line's shape is determined really by the way it sounds at its beginning and end, especially its end. It is here that the poet needs to make it 'come right' if he is not going to offend the ear. Reading our own poem aloud, even beating it out with a ruler on the table-edge as Yeats used to do, is not really good enough. The voice can hide any number of metrical shortcomings. That is why 'pub poems' are so often non-metrical when we write them down. We need to listen to our own poems with 'the inner ear' and, paradoxically, with the eye as well. We need to 'hear' how they arrive from the page.

The usual description of metre in feet is so unsatisfactory that it led Gerard Manley Hopkins to reject it altogether. He spoke merely of 'rising rhythm' (so-called iambs and anapaests) and 'falling rhythm' (so-called trochees and dactyls) according to the overall slope of the verse. This is sensible enough, and it does stop the 'scanner's' nonsense of saying, 'This is an anapaestic line with elisions' or 'an iambic line with extra light syllables'.

Yet basically this is what all lines are, or it is as good a way of describing them as any other. For the poet, it is a description not a prescription. It allows our brain to help our ear. The stricter the requirements of the form, the more we need metrical self-analysis.

A general practical guide is to say that the more unstressed syllables we drop into the line the more galloping, lighthearted (and often lightweight) it becomes. We do not quite speak in iambs, but we do not quite speak in free verse either. In this sense no verse is free. Because it has to be manufactured according to literary constraints, albeit indefinable ones, it is the hardest 'form' of all.

> Poetry lifts the veil from the hidden beauty of the world,
> and makes familiar objects be as if they were not familiar.
> Shelley *A Defence of Poetry*

2.

Most good poems are irregular, something quite different from 'free'. So, considered in detail, they seem to disregard the so-called rules of metre. What happens is that the poet works in 'metrical equivalents'. Nine, ten or eleven syllables seem to him capable of bearing the weight of an iambic pentameter. His ear has become so attuned to working with a given form that he writes not in but around it.

As a beginner, one tends to hold strictly to a metrical unit. It is this strictness which makes for dull verse. The rambling flower makes use of the trellis: it does not try to look like it.

If we decide to write syllabic verse, then everything I have said about scansion becomes irrelevant. We can develop our syllabics for ourselves on the basis of the writing exercise in chapter five. It is clear from that exercise that syllabics are a hard form, and they become even more difficult to manage, in spite of their metrical emancipation, if they make use of the stanzaic shapes that follow in later chapters; but strict stanzas, with rhyme, offer a way forward for the syllabic poet, and a powerful if less musical alternative to the tradition.

The syllabic proposition, which ignores a combination of number and stress to substitute number by itself — not five stressed intermixed with five unstressed syllables but ten syllables of any kind to a line — leads us back to another more ancient conundrum.

Words are not only stressed, they are made up of long and short syllables. That is, however we stress them, some things take longer to say than others. 'Moan' takes longer than 'man', though they both generally occupy a stressed position in verse or prose alike. In speech sometimes, and in verse more often, the stress can fall on a syllable which is shorter than the unstressed syllable next to it. To return to Browning's anapaests for a moment:

> 'Twas moonset at starting; but while we drew near
> Lockeren, the cocks crew and twilight dawned clear;
> At Boom a great yellow star came out to see . . .

How much longer is 'clear' than 'dawned'? Are we meant to give more weight (or length) to 'cocks' than 'crew'? Only because the metre says so.

Browning likes to confuse 'quick' rhythms with slow monosyllables. When we turn to polysyllables we find the language at large confusing. This arises principally from the disappearance of the secondary stress from many contemporary words. Until the late seventeenth century, and later in some parts of these islands, words of more than two syllables had a secondary stress — not 'príncipàllỹ' but 'príncipàllỹ'. If we try to *read* this word picked at random from the paragraph, it is almost impossible to stress it as we say it. The eye reminds us of the secondary stress. In speech, the modern Englishman, not Welshman, Irishman, Scotsman or American, solves the problem of the secondary stress in this word by getting rid of the syllable altogether, and pronouncing it 'princip'ly'.

A number of factors attend this suppression of the English secondary stress. One is that we have to resurrect it *against the contemporary bias* of the language if we wish polysyllables, of which there are a great number, to fit an iambic or trochaic metre. Since most metre is iambic, it is hard to make modern English sound natural in verse.

Then there is the difficulty, less expected, of matching contemporary English to the quantitative metres derived from Latin, the hexameter, for example. Who wants to? Well, it is clear that we have to look for some way forward. I for one would not like to be without Clough's *Amours de Voyage,* which save for short passages in Browning's blank verse and Whitman's free verse seems some of the most natural writing in nineteenth century poetry.

A third consequence is the separation of English and American prosody. American verse often sounds richer, more flexed, not because it is freer or truer to speech (though some is) — I think of mannered poets like Richard Wilbur — but because the secondary stress available to most Americans gives it a more muscular tension.

3.

Buried deeply in English and American is Old English or Anglo-Saxon. This is our parent language, the gut-tongue, not Latin and French; though these are the languages, with Italian, from which we derive most of our verse forms. Anglo-Saxon was not susceptible to these forms, and its own measures were eroded in the centuries after the Norman Conquest. Yet there was nothing inherently unsuitable about them that led to their demise in Modern English. They were flexible and adaptable to change. They simply could not compete with Chaucer's ability to fit Middle English to Continental measures. He was at court, and they were not. He was published by Caxton, and they were not. He was a prolific poet, as well as a very great one; whereas the century's two traditional poets of substantial stature did not leave us such a rich example. Chaucer's metrics remain with us today, even though the Middle English final 'e', one of the two factors — the other being the moribund secondary stress — that made his work possible, died almost as soon as he did.

It is this feeling about the unsuitability of regular stress, or regular length, to the way our language chimes that has led to the syllabic experiments, to free verse and to most of Hopkins' work. Sprung verse is not the same as the Old English metres, though, and the old form still needs to be given a proper chance by modern poets. It is entirely appropriate to the stressing of Modern American, and as near the stressing of contemporary English as are iambs and spondees, perhaps nearer. It is made up in half lines, each of two stresses, not more than two secondary stresses, and as many unstressed syllables as may be. In the nature of the language, this is not many.

A lot of modern poetry is already very near to it. When the early, more formal Hughes wrote:

A pig lay on a barrow, dead

he gave us the exact weight, without alliteration, of two Anglo-Saxon half-lines, that is, a full Anglo-Saxon line.

Festina lente
Suetonius

Chapter Eleven

I only knew one poet in my life:
And this, or something like it, was his way.

* * * * * * * * * *

He glanced o'er books on stalls with half an eye
And fly-leaf ballads on the vendor's string,
And broad-edged bold-print posters on the wall.
He took such cognizance of men and things,
If any beat a horse, you felt he saw;
If any cursed a woman, he took note;
Yet stared at nobody, — you stared at him.
Browning How It Strikes A Contemporary

1.

In the following pages I shall give the basic stanza forms available
to the poet. If a stanza form presupposes a given metre, I shall say
so. They are all susceptible to syllabics, and to the use of half-
rhymes and backrhymes.

Most of these forms will lie beyond, or behind, the poet's
immediate or envisaged needs. Practising them will be more in the
nature of play; but until we have turned all of the stones we shall
never know what is hidden under them.

Before then, we must look at a number of forms that do not
repeat their pattern in stanza units, or in some instances repeat
their pattern at all. The poet organises them simply into verse
paragraphs according to ear or common sense. Listed in rough
order of constraint these are: *free verse, Old English and Middle
English half-lines, hexameters, blank verse.* It is really a matter of
opinion whether or not the middle two are 'freer' than blank verse,
or whether they are governed by more flexible constraints.

2.

Only one person can teach us free verse. Ourself. It is an infinite
subject, more circumscribed by self-evolving limitations than any
other in prosody. Each poem makes its own fresh foray into the
diminishing possibilities of sound, and progress becomes more
difficult line by line and syllable by syllable.

Or if the sound of a line means anything to us, it does.

We should begin by reading *The Psalms* in the King James'
Bible, *The Song of Songs* and *Ezekiel.* Here we can find language
advanced beyond rhetoric into song, enhanced prose becoming
verse. Then we should look at Walt Whitman and D. H. Lawrence.
Both of them pose their problems and find their solutions:

Starting from fish-shape Paumanok where I was born,
Well-begotten, and raised by a perfect mother,
After roaming many lands, lover of populous pavements . . .
                    Walt Whitman *Starting from Paumanok*

Not every man has gentians in his house
in soft September, at slow, sad Michaelmas.

Bavarian gentians, big and dark, only dark
darkening the day-time torch-like with the smoking
    blueness of Pluto's gloom,
ribbed and torch-like, with their blaze of darkness
    spread blue
down flattening into points, flattened under the sweep
    of white day . . .
                    D. H. Lawrence *Bavarian Gentians*

Whitman is a poet of vast landscape and huge imperatives. Much
of his verse, like these lines from *Memories of President Lincoln,* is
finely wrought, composed while gazing upwards into the sun (his
arcane discipline):

in the swamp in secluded recesses,
A shy and hidden bird is warbling a song.

Solitary the thrush,
The hermit withdrawn to himself, avoiding the settlements,
Sings by himself a song . . .

But his larger resources are less in evidence, his ongoing metrical resources, that is. Whitman is primarily a poet of subject-matter. His verse bulges and breaks in its attempt to carry the pageant of expanding America. His theme, his fresh eye and his compassion are what makes him a great poet, not his prosody. He has no time for refinement; or rather his refinements, subtle and deliberate though they are, are usually at the beginning of a poem. He is validating himself with his reader before presenting the weight of his after-statement in the form of a list or a chant, generally both:

On the beach at night alone,
As the old mother sways her to and fro singing her husky song,
As I watch the bright stars shining, I think
a thought of the clef of the universe and of the future.

A vast similitude interlocks all,
All spheres, grown, ungrown, small, large, suns, moons, planets,
All distances of place however wide,
All distances of time, all inanimate forms,
All souls, all living bodies . . .

It is not being dismissive of Whitman to say that he has advanced the 'list poem' to its highest level. Nor must we forget that he was the pioneer of free verse, and a nineteenth century poet. His occasional unhappy moments occur, as with Wordsworth, when his highly personal diction is penetrated by the more traditional styles he seeks to exclude.

If our themes are big enough, as they were for Ginsberg in *Howl,* then Whitman is an adequate model: a well-turned opening followed by a selective, carefully organised list — rich in images, but a list nonetheless.

Lawrence offers a better way forward, I think. In *Bavarian Gentians,* the poem quoted above, he counterpoints comparatively facile repetition with a rich sense of assonance (sound echoing sound). More than that, though, there is the matter of his imagery. Lawrence's images always work because they reflect not merely, or not primarily, his imaginative insights but his decision. He *decided* what the gentians meant to him, the images follow that decision. The assonances follow the images, and the rhetoric, shallow without them, turns on the other three and triumphs.

Lawrence's most striking poems are nearly all poems of movement, though: *Bat, Mountain Lion, Snake.* The last named is a good poem to use as a model because it tells a story. If we have a story to tell, then free verse is a good medium. The verse trims the rubbish from the story; the story cuts away the clutter that attends early attempts at verse.

Lawrence offers us something else. Rage. Many of his poems are written from anger or frustration. They come straight out like a stream of invective because that is what they are. The verse rides on itself just as oaths ride on themselves.

So if we write in white heat, or from clear conviction, then we may find our poems falling happily into free verse. If we wish to experiment in free verse then it is better to find stories to tell than to philosophise about logs or railway lines.

In any event we should read Rexroth, Ferlinghetti, Henri, Patten and, more particularly because of their sheer craftsmanship as well as their imaginative weight, Hughes and Redgrove.

> I had read him all over before I was twelve years old, and was thus made a Poet.
>
> Abraham Cowley *Of Myself*

All of these people in their various ways *sing*. Free verse like all verse must sing. When we write it we must pen it in our ear and taste it in our mouth.

The most simple way to understand is to copy a newspaper article, breaking the sentences into verse-lengths, then alter it until it sings. We may never make it work as free verse, but at the end we shall know a lot more about the boundary between verse and prose.

3.

The Anglo-Saxons wrote in a highly wrought, artificial form governed by intricate precedence and lumbered, in part, by a poetic diction that even stylised the imagery. Yet, as I noted in an earlier chapter, it remains close to the genius of the language, especially to modern American, or to dialects that keep the secondary stress.

Let me ill-do the opening of *The Wanderer* very roughly into a modern equivalent:

> Often the Wanderer   wins God's blessing
> his Saviour's mercy   though moodily he journeys
> rowing raw-handed   the rime-clenched sea

The pattern is two stresses in each half-line, with each stress supported by not more than one secondary stress, and — in theory but never in practice — any number of unstressed syllables. There is too much grit in the verse movement for it to tolerate the leaven of many light syllables. A stress (as in 'wins') may stand by itself, though the other foot in the half-line is generally made heavy by the ballast of a strong secondary stress, as here.

The other constraint, relatively unimportant, is the alliteration (underlined above). Both stresses in the first half-line (if not both, then the second only) alliterate with the first stress in the second. There is no reason why a modern poet should alliterate, or alliterate that strictly; and no reason at all why the ugly break should be shown in the typography.

I take it that the Anglo-Saxon measure was exactly what Jenny Joseph meant in a poem which begins:

> One summer Sunday similar to others . . .

It moves very easily and unobtrusively.

By the fourteenth century, the line was even more relaxed, too much so according to some commentators. Yet it was the metre of the *Gawain* poet, and of the poet we call Langland. Alliteration, and unstressed syllables, proliferate to give us a lighter model.

> In the Summer season when the sun shone softly
> I robed myself in rags as though I were a shepherd . . .

The two great anonymous alliterative poets provide us with a fine template. So does Dunbar in his robust early-Sixteenth Century poem *The Twa Maryit Women and the Wedo*

. . . and not say that Poetry abuseth man's wit, but that man's wit abuseth Poetry.
Sir Philip Sidney *Apologie for Poetrie*

In theory the hexameter is ponderous with artifice. If we judge it quantitatively from Latin scansion and serve ourselves a basket of dactyls and spondees weighed in *long* and *short* syllables then it will be a dire feast.

So let us consider it as a six-*stressed* line, in origin five dactyls followed by a spondee. Precedence says that any dactyl except the fifth may have a spondee substituted for it. Common sense in English allows us to use trochees instead of spondees, and sheer cussedness reminds us that an elided dactyl is a spondee anyway.

Once we have said all of that we need do no more than listen to a good example. Here is ancient Clough in *Amóurs de Voyage* being sexist but modern:

Am I prepared to lay down my life for the British female?
Really, who knows? One has bowed and talked, till, little by little,
All the natural heat has escaped of the chivalrous spirit.
Oh, one conformed, of course; but one doesn't die for good manners,
Stab, or shoot, or be shot, by way of graceful attention.
No, if it should be at all, it should be on the barricades there;
Should I incarnadine ever this inky pacifical finger,
Sooner should it be for this vapour of Italy's freedom,
Sooner far by the side of the dam'd and dirty plebians.
Ah, for a child in the street I could strike; for the full-blown lady —
Somehow, Eustace, alas! I have not felt the vocation.

It is often objected that something dumpish and brutish about the hexameter's ending makes enjambment (lines running on to the next) impossible. Not for our hoary old modernistic model:

Rome disappoints me much; I hardly as yet understand, but
Rubbishy seems the word that most exactly would suit it . . .
It is a blessing, no doubt, to be rid, at least for a time, of
All one's friends and relations, — yourself (forgive me!) included,
All the *assujettisement* of having been what one has been . . .

5.

With blank verse we approach the centre of the mystery. No matter how passionately we argue that free verse or the derivatives of the Anglo-Saxon four-stressed metre are closest to the genius of the language, nor how persuasively we make a case for the future of syllabics, the fact remains that for the six hundred years since it was given such massive impetus by Chaucer one line length and one rhythm have lain at the heart of English poetry: the five-stressed iambic line, or iambic pentameter. Blank Verse, the unrhymed pentameter, was not current until the sixteenth century, when it became established as the natural verse for drama. We have had it ever since, in many moods and voices, for it is flexible almost beyond comparison.

Its basis may be best understood by looking at it early in its career. Here is Marlowe, well able to move line into line, but thinking nonetheless in multiples of five-stressed units:

> One thing, good servant, let me crave of thee,
> To glut the longing of my heart's desire,
> That I might have unto my paramour,
> That heavenly Helen which I saw of late,
> Whose sweet imbracings may extinguish cleane
> These thoughts that do disswade me from my vow,
> And keepe mine oath I made to Lucifer.

In Shakespeare's hands, the end-stopped movement is varied by mid-line stops, by feminine endings, by the treatment of proper names as extra-metrical; and above all by an instinct towards slabs of sound that have a metrical equivalent, rather than following the iambic thump too exactly. Such a verse is much more suited to the needs of drama:

> Faith, he is posted hence on serious matter.
> It was great ignorance, Gloucester's eyes being out,
> To let him live: where he arrives he moves
> All hearts against us: Edmund, I think, is gone
> In pity of his misery, to dispatch
> His nighted life; moreover to descry
> The strength o' the army.

Shakespeare's language is theatrical; but it is his example as a poet — albeit in the context of his plays — that has so profoundly influenced subsequent developments. In copying Shakespeare, many lesser writers have forgotten the underlying dynamic of his work:

> It will have blood; they say, blood will have blood:
> Stones have been known to move and trees to speak;
> Augures and understood relations have
> By maggot-pies and choughs and rooks brought forth
> The secret'st man of blood . . . What is the night?

> Almost at odds with morning.

The blank verse poets, particularly the later pastoralist of the eighteenth and nineteenth century, overlooked the fact that Shakespeare's verse became more highly charged as the dramatic voltage increased. There is a frame of action and emotion surrounding everything he wrote. It is part of his genius that the frame and the picture become inseparable; but there is really no point in writing blank verse unless we have such a frame or its equivalent. As Doctor Johnson warned us, we must expect to astonish, or stay away from blank verse altogether.

He was writing of Milton, who did astonish by the weight of his intellect, the breadth of his vision and by his Latinate, almost aureate diction. Milton brought action and emotion to his poetry, and a sensational though contentious form of embellishment. It was this embellished diction, so suited to his own needs and so much at odds with the requirement of his successors, that was to clog the development of blank verse for a century and a half. Even Wordsworth, great innovator though he was, does not entirely escape Milton's influence. The young Keats first basked in it, then felt himself destroyed by it.

Of course, the intending poet will read *The Prelude* and discover for himself what music it makes in its great passages, particularly early on. Presumably, too, *The Lines Written Above Tintern Abbey* are required reading for us all. If we care for blank verse and believe it has a role to play in our own work, then we shall be better off neglecting Milton and his eighteenth century imitators, and rubbing much Shakespeare against some Browning. There is no one contemporary for us to look at. Frost always strikes me as dull when he sloughs off rhyme.

Perhaps blank verse is dead, and the life is to be found earlier in the chapter.

Their works drop groundwards, but themselves, I know,
Reach many a time a heaven that's shut to me . . .

Speak as they please, what does the mountain care? . . .

Ah, but a man's reach should exceed his grasp,
Or what's a heaven for?

Browning *Andrea del Sarto*
(called 'The Faultless Painter')

Chapter Twelve

Physics of metaphysic begs defence,
And metaphysic calls for aid on sense!
See mystery to mathematics fly!
In vain! They gaze, turn giddy, rave and die.
Religion blushing veils her sacred fires,
And unawares morality expires.
For public flame, nor private, dares to shine,
Nor human spark is left, nor glimpse divine!
Lo! thy dread empire, Chaos, is restored;
Light dies before thy uncreating word;
Thy hand, great Anarch, lets the curtain fall.
And universal darkness buries all.

Alexander Pope *The Dunciad*

1.

The couplet is, if you like, rhymed blank verse. The heroic couplet is end-stopped rhymed blank verse. Chaucer was more flexible in couplets before the heroic age. Only minor poets have been so since, though in this century Roy Campbell and Martin Skinner have given the form an extended run.

Poets should read Dryden and Pope to discover its range, and Chaucer to remind themselves of its lyric and dramatic flexibility. The way forward must surely be with more virtuosity in rhyme and rhythm. Louis MacNeice points ahead in his *Eclogues,* but not quite in iambic pentameters. Indeed, he soon switches altogether; but a nod is as good as a wink:

A. I meet you in an evil time.
B.   The evil bells
   Put out of our heads, I think, the thought of
                                    everything else.
A. The jaded calendar revolves,
   Its nuts need oil, carbon chokes the valves,
   The excess sugar of a diabetic culture
   Rotting the nerve of life and literature.

Put this with *The Dunciad:* there is our template.

The heroic or elegaic quatrain is the same measure opened out into a four-line stanza, the first line rhyming with the third, the second with the fourth. Gray's *Elegy* is the most famous example:

> The Curfew tolls the knell of parting day,
> The lowing herd winds slowly o'er the lea,
> The plowman homeward plods his weary way,
> And leaves the world to darkness and to me.

But the quatrain need not be so heroic:

> My tattered battledress, moth-eaten at the crotch
> Hangs in the cupboard, adding to its sores;
> Still creased, of course: I never soldiered much
> Nor wore my private ballsache to the wars.

I gain the bounce, the note of sinister bonhommie, by being extra-metrical at the beginning of the verse (or by calling up the Alexandrine, or six-stress variant, which is always available to the heroic tradition?). Certainly the pentameter becomes more acceptable to the modern ear if we add one or two light syllables to the line.

3.

The heroic quatrain forms the basis of the Shakespearean sonnet, which consists of three quatrains followed by a couplet. The quatrains may be quite separate, in which case the sonnet is indeed called Shakespearean, or they may be linked each to the next by means of through-rhymes, in which case they are called Spenserian. Shakespeare and Spenser did not invent either form, but they gave each of them an airing in extended sonnet sequences which we should read and learn from. The sonnet has been well handled recently by Auden and George Barker.

Here is the pure form (well? — one feminine ending) as exemplified by Shakespeare:

> When in disgrace with Fortune and men's eyes,
> I all alone beweep my outcast state,
> And trouble deaf heaven with my bootless cries,
> And look upon myself and curse my fate,
> Wishing me like to one more rich in hope,
> Featured like him, like him with friends possessed,

Desiring this man's art, and that man's scope,
With what I most enjoy contented least,
Yet in these thoughts my self almost despising,
Haply I think on thee, and then my state,
(Like to the lark at break of day arising
From sullen earth) sings hymns at heaven's gate,
For thy sweet love remembered such wealth brings,
That then I scorn to change my state with kings.

The other main dynasty of sonnet is the Petrarchan. Older, more sonorous and more intricate, it has an entirely different flavour. The Spenserian/Shakespearean form is witty and epigrammatic. It gathers itself for a final thrust with its couplet. The Petrarchan form is mellow and philosophical (though John Donne uses it to gust up philosophy till it blows like a tempest), dividing itself between an opening eight lines of exposition, the *octave*, and a final six lines of conclusion, the *sestet*. At their purest, the two forms have in common only their length of a hundred and forty syllables.

The Petrarchan through-rhymes two *In Memoriam* quatrains, strictly using only two rhymes: *abba abba;* then it through-rhymes its last six lines in any combination of two or three rhymes, providing that it does not end in a couplet, common permutations being: *cddcdc*; *cddccd*; *cdcdcd*; or, on three rhymes, *cdecde*; *cdeedc*; and, less usually, *cddeec*.

Milton and Wordsworth are the great traditional exponents of the Petrarchan form, though they both have their eccentricities (and why not?). Wordsworth likes as full a variety of rhymes as possible, and Milton almost invariably runs the octave into the sestet. To catch this sonnet at its purest, we *should* read Milton's *When The Assault Was Intended To The City*.

Instead let him and the seventeenth century point the way forward with:

A book was writ of late called *Tetrachordon*,
And woven close, both matter, form and style;
The subject new, it walked the town a while,
Numbering good intellects: now seldom pored on.
Cries the stall-reader, 'Bless us! what a word on
A title-page is this!'; and some in file
Stand spelling false, while one might walk to Mile —
End Green. Why is it harder, sirs, than *Gordon*,
Colkitto, or *Macdonnel*, or *Galasp*?

Those rugged names to our like mouths grow sleek,
That would have made Quintilian stare and gasp.
Thy age, like ours, O soul of Sir John Cheek,
Hated not learning worse than toad or asp,
When thou taught'st Cambridge and King Edward Greek

This is remarkably modern in flavour, and instructive as an example. I am sure that John Berryman, himself a Petrarchan, made something of it in *Berryman's Sonnets:*

Sigh as it ends . . . I keep an eye on your
Amour with Scotch, — too *cher* to consummate;
Faster your disappearing beer than late-
ly mine; your naked passion for the floor;
Your hollow leg; your hanker for one more
Dark as the Sundam Trench; how you dilate
Upon psychotics of this class, collate
Stages, and . . . how long since you, well, *forbore.*

Ah, but the high fire sings on to be fed
Whipping our darkness by the lifting sea
A while, O darling drinking like a clock.
The tide comes on: spare, Time, from what you spread
Her story, — tilting a frozen Daiquiri
Blonde, barefoot, beautiful,
flat on the bare floor rivetted to Bach.

Berryman very rarely allows himself the extra-metrical excess of that last line, and he respects the division between octave and sestet. But the sonnet is a living form, and it thrives equally well on irregularities and hybridisation.

The most usual cross-breed consists of two Shakespearean quatrains followed by a three-rhymed sestet. It combines the most relaxed attributes of both forms. Rilke's *Sonnette an Orpheus* are worth examining in this respect. Even without speaking German we can pick up his rhyme-scheme, his shifts of metre, and his drastic alteration of line length. He reminds us that the sonnet is not a fossil. In any event, J. B. Leishman has translated him with great metrical fidelity:

Inter-stellar spaces — ah, yes, but how many times greater
spaces terrestial are!
First, for example, a child . . . then a neighbour,
a moment later, —
oh, how incredibly far!

Fate but through spanning us, maybe, with Being's measure
seems so strange to our eyes:
think of the spans to a man from a maid, whose pleasure
lingers with him she flies!

All is remote — nowhere does the circle close.
Look at that curious face on the welcoming table,
staring out of its dish.

Fishes are dumb . . . so one imagined. Who knows?
May there not be some place where, *without* them, the
                    dwellers are able
to speak what would be the language of fish?

> Now no one indeed supposes that the chicken does what
> it does with the same self-consciousness with which a
> tailor makes a suit of clothes. Not any one who has thought
> upon the subject is likely to do it so great an injustice . . . It
> works with such absolute certainty and so vast an
> experience, that it is utterly incapable of following the
> operations of its own mind.
>
>   Samuel Butler *Life and Habit*

4.

Rilke brings us a long way from the iambic pentameter, and a good
thing too. We mentioned the *In Memoriam* stanza earlier, though;
and that consists of four iambic tetrameters rhyming *abba*, a sort of
sandwich quatrain:

> How fares it with the happy dead?
> For here the man is more and more;
> But he forgets the days before
> God shut the doorways of his head.

It was Tennyson who made this measure, and it does seem to have
died with him.
  Giving an occasional flourish is the Omar Khayyam quatrain.

This rhymes *aaba,* and the trailing unrhymed line does enhance the muscularity of the metre:

> For in the Marketplace, one Dusk of Day,
> I watch'd the Potter thumping his wet Clay:
> And with its all obliterated Tongue
> It murmur'd — 'Gently, Brother, gently, pray!'

Fitzgerald's punctuation, and his archaisms, are to be avoided. That being said, this remains a good form for anyone wishing to write a sequence of epigrammatic or aphoristic pieces.

Strictly, of course, any four-line verse is a quatrain. The ballad we practised in an earlier chapter is a quatrain, even though it alternates four- and three-stressed lines rhyming either *abab* or *abcb.* The four-stressed line can also have an interior rhyme, the second stress rhyming with the fourth stress.

Quatrains too are the Long Measure and Short Measure of the hymn books. The Long Measure is four four-stressed lines, rhyming *abab* or *abcb.* The Short Measure rhymes similarly but has two three-stressed lines followed by a four-stressed and then a three-stressed line. All three of these shorter-line forms tend to be irregular in stress; and the ballad, being an early folk-song measure, can be prolific with light syllables. The two hymn measures are perhaps best expressed as syllabics, since the mathematics of more modern (and sedate) music insist that sums take precedence over stress.

5.

We have stepped away from the pentameter in order to be fair to the quatrain. It is worth remembering that these 'shorter' measures are in fact derived from longer units which once flourished, and which are probably still instinctive with us. The ballad started as a broken seven-stressed couplet, and if we wish to use it (it is easily the most simple rhyming form available to us) then we should teach our ear to listen to it at length rather than in little. So, too, with the hymn measures which disguise an ancient dance rhythm, though they rarely dance today.

If we can trace the evolution of a measure we can often unlock it for ourselves and make it useful to us.

Back now to pentameters with the *terza rima, ottava rima* and *Spenserian stanza,* fancy verses all of them, but far from defunct.

The *terza rima,* with its syllabic and assonated relatives, is the most lively of them all. It rhymes *aba bcb cdc,* and so on, like a madman's sandwich or a piece of packaged angel cake. Strictly it should end with a couplet, since even a maniac runs out of stuffing eventually; and this leads to an interesting consideration: four of its triplets plus couplet *aba bcb cdc ded ee* ring up a .pleasing variation of the Spenserian sonnet, so that, for instance, it becomes a moot point as to whether Shelley's *Ode To The West Wind* is five paragraphs of *terza rima* or five linked sonnets.

Who cares? I think we all should, because it is a cool little measure that spawns in the brain, perhaps because of its typographic attractiveness. Before singing its praises further, I should like to note that it can be ended, by the visually tidy and by couplet-haters, *xyx yxy,* that is by turning the rhyme of the last triplet back on itself.

The form is caught from Dante, of course; and its Italian origins often persuade it to use extra light syllables, stressed syllabics (four stresses in a ten syllable line), and double, even triple rhymes or assonances. Shelley and Byron both used it, Shelley most interestingly in *The Triumph of Life,* the poem he was writing the day that he drowned; and then Browning picked it up and used it *as a narrative measure* in *The Statue And The Bust.* He thus returned it to its Dante-esque origins and somehow pushed it into the twentieth century.

Poets as different as Robert Frost, Robert Graves, Roy Fuller and Charles Madge have adopted it for a variety of different purposes; but its real impetus lies, I think, in its aforementioned visual qualities. Interestingly the four poets listed have all written in other triplet forms, using everything from triple rhymes (the pure triplet) to, in the case of Madge and Graves, no rhyme at all.

Nor should we dismiss its visual and metrical relationship with that most indestructible of all artificial forms, the *villanelle.* This consists of five or more (usually five) tercets (clusters of three lines) followed by a quatrain. The tercets rhyme *aba aba* (repeat), so the whole poem is written on two rhyming sounds. However, the first line of the first tercet is repeated at the end of the second and fourth tercet, and as the third line of the quatrain. The last line of the first tercet is repeated at the end of the third and fifth tercet, and then as the last line of the quatrain.

I have before me, five advanced grammar books whose days have retreated. They all consign the villanelle to a mausoleum where they suggest it should be interred with the remains of Ernest Dowson and Austin Dobson. All I wish to observe is that this venerable form has enhanced the pages of Auden and Empson, and to remind the reader of its complications by quoting *Do not go gentle into that good night.* one of those poems by Dylan Thomas that are so good that we tend to forget what shape they make to the eye and ear:

> Do not go gentle into that good night,
> Old age should burn and rave at close of day;
> Rage, rage against the dying of the light.
>
> Though wise men at their end know dark is right,
> Because their word has forked no lightning they
> Do not go gentle into that good night.
>
> Good men, the last wave by, crying how bright
> Their frail deeds might have danced in a green bay,
> Rage, rage against the dying of the light.
>
> Wild men who caught and sang the sun in flight,
> And learn, too late, they grieved it on its way,
> Do not go gentle into that good night.
>
> Grave men, near death, who see with blinding sight
> Blind eyes could blaze like meteors and be gay,
> Rage, rage against the dying of the light.
>
> And you, my father, there on the sad height,
> Curse, bless, me now with your fierce tears, I pray.
> Do not go gentle into that good night.
> Rage, rage against the dying of the light.

The two most common rhyme-sounds of the sixteenth and seventeenth century, *night* and *day,* are here carried by the form and by the passion (certainly not by the intellect). Dowson's villanelles were rightly consigned to a dark place, but then they were light in line. The form seems to require the iambic pentameter or its metrical or syllabic equivalent.

Note to the test tube poet: *quantity* as well as quality or stress is important here; the *spondee* works rather than decorates.

... to have written well in verse, yea and in small parcels, deserveth great praise ...
Richard Tottel, Preface to the *Miscellany*

The *ottava rima* seems to have become a satirists' platter, perhaps because *abababcc* needs a lot of enjambment, wit-rhyme and split-rhyme to make it work. Byron set it up for us in *Don Juan,* or rather he taught us the tone:

> His afternoons he pass'd in visits, luncheons,
> Lounging, and boxing; and the twilight hour
> In riding round those vegetable puncheons
> Call'd 'Parks', where there is neither fruit nor flower,
> Enough to gratify a bee's slight munchings;
> But, after all, it is the only 'bower'
> (In Moore's phrase) where the fashionable fair
> Can form a slight acquaintance with fresh air.

No one else has really taken up the challenge. Elsewhere it had died with Keats, and not been properly born among the Cockneys (who used it) before Byron wrote the above lines.

This is a pity.

The Spenserian stanza, well used by Keats in *The Eve Of St. Agnes* and by Byron in *Childe Harold's Pilgrimage,* seems to have less to offer. It consists of eight iambic pentameters and one six-stressed line, or Alexandrine. The rhyme is *ababbcbcc.* I have seen some very arid syllabic variants. Spenser, who invented it, allowed himself the linguistic flexibility (and the fuller rhyming resources) of a fake archaism.

Spenser developed his stanza from the perfectly good Rhyme Royal of Chaucer's *Troilus and Cresseyde,* which rhymes, with or without Alexandrine, *ababbcc.* This and its variants have been used by Masefield in various of his book-length narratives, and by Auden in his *Letter to Lord Byron* where he surprisingly enough passes over the Byronic *ottava rima* while aping the tone:

> . . . With notes from perfect strangers starting, 'Sir,
> I like your lyrics, but *Childe Harold's* trash,'
> 'My daughter writes, should I encourage her?'
> Sometimes containing frank demands for cash,
> Sometimes sly hints at a platonic pash,
> And sometimes, though I think this rather crude,
> The correspondent's photo in the nude.

The most usual variant of this metre is the one which gets rid of the couplets: *ababcbc;* but it is also possible to retain two couplets while separating them: *abbabcc;* and there is a three couplet version: *abbaacc.*

103

6.

The *sestina* is a dull thing. Most modern poets have tried their
hands, or feet at it, as they should. Unfortunately, some have
published the results. Yet it remains a useful form, both for the
metrical and the syllabic poet.

Its first interest for us is that it presents a genuine substitute for
rhyme on a basis of word-permutation. Perhaps that is why so
many sestinas read rather like a football pool. Six six-line
unrhyming stanzas of pentametric weight and each of their lines
with the same words and in the order in which they appear in the
first stanza, save that the first line of the first stanza becomes the
last line of the second, the first line of the second becomes the last
line of the third, and so on. The first served goes to the back of the
queue and the rest each move up a place. Then there is a final
tercet, or three-line verse, which either operates on the next three
words in order, or on the key word principle (this is a form of
muddied antecedents and dubious precedents). There is a tradition
in English that these words should be noticeable and preferably
polysyllabics or compounds. Thus the resulting poem has a
lugubrious end-stopped feeling about it.

Clearly the six words must be chosen with enormous care. We
are going to hear each of them six times, and three of them seven
times. They need to be the words that sum up the theme, the
message and the imaginative fibre of the poem, so that in a sense
each sestina contains its own cypher, its own short-hand version.

Or we have to find a way to kick those words out of the window
or camouflage them as a functional part of the frame. We can do
the former, make them disappear, by selecting less obvious words,
including relatives and conjunctions, and crafting them into the
enjambment of freely flowing lines. The latter can be achieved by
following the French tradition and making our six key words
rhyme on an *ababab* basis. They will then bow to the usual
pressures governing rhyme words and be neither too opaque nor
too transparent. The tercet should either bring up the next three
words in order, which will automatically rhyme *aba* to the *b* of the
last line of the last stanza, or it should select key words which fit
the same pattern.

Ezra Pound gives us the basic modern example in *Altaforte*. Swinburne has a fine rhyming example written in French in *Poems and Ballads (Second Series)*. George Barker has had one or two playfully half-hearted attempts at the real thing, and he points the way towards some useful variants without developing them. It seems to me perfectly acceptable that an end word like *pavement* should metamorphose to *paving, cement* or even *sidewalk* (all mine, not the excesses of the excessive George), that *backwards* should become *forwards* and *entrails,* because the first point of a sestina (or any other poem) is to keep its reader awake.

Surely, too, this is a form which cries out for ongoing, or developing, assonances or backrhymes? There are only two backrhymes in each word, but a well-chosen word can be turned inside-out in more ways than two, notably by a combination of anagram and backrhymes.

This is becoming too much like a crossword puzzle? Remember: it only started out as a football pool.

7.

The sestina is ill-done and overdone. The *ballade,* on the other hand, is not done at all. I never read Villon, whether in the original or in the Anglo-American versions of his more gutsy translators, without thinking that this is a pity. Metres may vary, so may rhyme schemes, provided that certain basic criteria are met. It is the presidency of these inflexibles over a host of variables that make it such an attractive form.

There must be three stanzas only of eight or ten lines each, followed by an *envoy,* more in the way of a summation than a summary, of four or five lines, according to whether it follows an eight-line or a ten-line stanza.

Three or four rhymes only must be used, again according to stanza length, and the stanza form must be consistent throughout the poem. The rhyming words must either repeat throughout the poem, rather as in a sestina but without rolling forward, or they must through-rhyme. So if the first line of the first verse ends in *fire,* then so must the first line of the second and third verse, or they must rhyme say *fire, pyre, lyre.*

The envoy, normally only half the length of the stanza, generally picks up the rhyme pattern, and indeed the metric arrangement, of the second part of the stanza. The poem's sense of anguish, complaint or vituperation is further reinforced by a refrain, the last line of the first verse ending both the other two verses and the envoy. I put it as woodenly as that, because in some forms the refrain is a kind of additive. Not in the *ballade*. It is part of the structure and argument and therefore the syntax of the verse.

8.

We have not only turned stones; we have crept under them. Forgive me for not trying to crawl beneath the remaining grains of sand. I enjoy the *rondeau* and the *rondels* of Villon, and the two or three rondeaux of Chaucer and Wyatt. I know of no serious poet who is trying to write them seriously today. Anyone who plays with the villanelle will find them eventually.

The *Chant Royal* is a longer and more elaborate form of *ballade*, having five stanzas of eleven lines, and an envoy of from five to eight lines. It is visible in early modern French, and probably lives on in some of the louche street songs in which their culture is so rich and ours so poor. The Romance languages are much better suited to forms that require a constantly refurbished rhyme than is our own. Multiple rhymes very quickly reduce poetry to farce. An English poet who wants to cut his teeth on wit already has plenty to bite on.

It's a naked child against a hungry wolf;
It's playing bowls upon a splitting wreck;
It's walking on a string across a gulf
With millstones fore-and-aft about your neck . . .
John Davidson *Thirty Bob A Week*

Then I must remember that there are people who make poems by cutting words from novels and newspapers, tearing the Queensland Malaria Report in half or jotting down the advertisements that come angelically borne by buses; there are random poets and trance-writers, men and women whose work is dictated by a medium or control, and those who are in daily contact with Homer and Keats, even with Longfellow. I congratulate them all and confess I have nothing concrete in the way of advice to hand them.

My hope is to help, directly or indirectly, those who want to *make* poems. However exaggerated the claims we advance for the products of our inspiration we should not allow ourselves to forget that a poem is always, at the least, a piece of literature. Sometimes